CULTURAL PLURALISM
and the
AMERICAN IDEA

With comments by Stanley H. Chapman,
Stewart G. Cole, Elizabeth F. Flower,
Frank P. Graham, R. J. Henle, S.J.,
Herold C. Hunt, Milton R. Konvitz,
Leo Pfeffer, and Goodwin Watson

PHILADELPHIA

UNIVERSITY OF PENNSYLVANIA PRESS

CULTURAL PLURALISM
and the
AMERICAN IDEA

An Essay in Social Philosophy

by **HORACE M. KALLEN**

PREFACE

In the spring of 1954, Professor Horace M. Kallen of the New School for Social Research was invited by the Albert M. Greenfield Center for Human Relations of the University of Pennsylvania to deliver two lectures on Cultural Pluralism. These lectures were planned as the basis for the present volume, which was also to include contributions by specialists in various disciplines who would comment critically on what Professor Kallen said. Then, in the concluding section, he would reply to these critics.

The lectures were revised by Professor Kallen and mimeographed. They were then sent to a group of scholars who had agreed to participate in the undertaking. Unfortunately, some of them found that the pressure of their duties did not enable them to meet the designated deadline. Several others were in such agreement with the author that they decided not to submit papers, because their comments would not add significantly to the volume. Two others wrote critical letters, which Professor Kallen has taken account of in his concluding statement. He has also added some footnotes.

This volume is the first in a series which the Albert M. Greenfield Center for Human Relations proposes to issue as its *Studies in Human Relations*. Its publication is made possible by a generous subvention of Mr. Albert M. Greenfield, whose interest and support has made the Center for Human Relations possible.

Martin P. Chworowsky
Director

CONTENTS

I

CULTURAL PLURALISM
AND THE AMERICAN IDEA

OF MEANINGS OF CULTURE

by Horace M. Kallen

To such as are alert to the voices of our times, the word "culture" speaks with various meanings. There are meanings which alone our eggheads hatch out and nurture in the form of letters, music, architecture, the graphic and plastic arts. There are meanings which mostly our boneheads fertilize and cherish. There are meanings religious and meanings secular, meanings projected as the conservation of values, and meanings attained in the works and ways of the sciences of nature and the sciences of man. Every one of those meanings of culture compounds into our ideas of what a human being is or isn't. Some inform man with culture as a quality inborn and dynamically constitutive. Others determine him as an animal born and merely nursed and nurtured into that cultural singularity we distinguish as human.

Certainly, only some types of insects and some of the simpler varieties of monocellular organisms share with the *genus humanum* the capacity to increase and to multiply, to live and to thrive almost anywhere on the globe. Certainly no mammal does. Mankind's dwelling places are as diverse as the regions and climates of the earth, and the forms and figures of his dwellings are so much more so, that their differences from one another are far more impressive than their similarities. Yet, however signal these differences, they diverge from a basic mammalian congruence which enables males and females of any region to mate and breed with those of any other. However easy or arduous the upkeep and transmission of any singularity of form and figure, they shape up the struggles of a psychosomatic mammalian organization whose basic activities can be accounted for as repetitions of one another, regardless of their alterations and multitude. Sciences of man refer them to primal identities without whose postulation the sciences could not be sciences; and certain philosophies signalize such identities as "the human condition"; the condition, they contend, constitutes the humanity of mankind; our cultures are its consequence, not its essence. Like other zoölogical kinds, mankind are a race of animals; the humanity of man, no less than the protozoity of protozoa, is a biological process, accounted for and understood in the degree that its simplest components are discerned and the trajectories of their ongoing combinations and separations traced, mapped, and coded in laws.

The number and variety of social sciences which discourse upon such laws multiply with the years. We may count political science, economics, sociology, anthropology, social psychology, history; and we may count diversifications of these disciplines effected by the prefixing of "cultural" as a characterizing epithet. To these is now joined another discipline, purporting to concern itself with culture, as Hegel might say, *an und für sich*, by itself and for itself, culture "as such." Its apostles and practitioners call this new discipline "culturology." Each of the many communions of culture study is distinguished by new expressions devised *ad hoc* by its initiates. Each varies the intent of the word "culture" with new shades of meaning, which presently neither time nor space permits to bring into the conspectus of this discussion. I shall here treat only of a few which impress me as conveying the more significant variations.

I

The most widespread and most consequential meaning of "culture" would obviously be the customary one among the rank and file of citizens struggling every day for a livelihood and a life rather than that conventional among professional specialists of the arts or the social sciences, or among the amateur connoisseurs who practice them with virtuosity.

Most of us men and women, whatever our age, pass the waking hours of the day in a factory, a field, a mine, a shop, an office, a schoolroom, a hospital, a church, or other specific place having a characteristic architecture, layout, furniture, tools and other equipment. They are the places where we work at our trades, practice our professions so as to earn our livings. By our relations to them, and by our use of their furniture and equipment we know ourselves and are known to our friends, to our neighbors, to the census takers and the pollsters, as farmers, cowboys, miners, shoemakers, tailors, shirtmakers, typists, carpenters, barbers, teachers, doctors, lawyers, ministers, newsmen, firemen, policemen, soldiers, congressmen, un-American committeemen, and so on down. Many of our occupations acquire not only characteristic tools and equipment but also characteristic dress: uniforms, badges, and other devices whereby we are recognized as earning our living thiswise and not thatwise. There are communities which customarily distinguish not only occupations, but social status, caste, class, race and rank, by means of dress, as well as tattoo marks, medals, ribbons and other insignia.

Dress serves not only as a criterion of difference, but as a signal of identification. It is the visible feather which first draws the flocking birds together. Whether it is a coverall of the whole person, or simply a badge with a number and a photograph, it is a ticket of admission and a sign of belonging. And in great industrial plants this belonging, whether determined by the operation performed, the craft practiced or the total industry, is imposed by the configuration of the plant and the character of its equipment. It is not chosen by the hand who receives a place at which he operates a tool. The operative, earning his living, is not engaged in free enterprise among companions of his own choice, at his own risk. His place is predetermined by his specific assignment in a division of labor already prescribed by the structure of the automatic machine at which he operates, or the conveyor system which determines what operation he shall repeat, how, and when, and how often he shall repeat it, during the eight hours of his working day. His companions in work are in the same case. They may be entire strangers to one another, yet each is dependent on all others for the performance of an operation without which the production of the commodity from whose sale their wages derive could not be completed. Trade-union members or not, this interdependence of theirs, determined by the sequential pattern made by the moving parts of a stationary machine, or the ordered tempo of a conveyor system, is imposed, not chosen. No operative is himself a craftsman making a whole shoe, a whole shirt, a whole automobile or a whole anything. He is only a fraction of such a craftsman—1/200 or 1/500 of such a craftsman. The complete craftsman is the factory.

This, with its structure and equipment, whereof the human beings affixed to them and detached from them may be counted as so many biological machine parts, is the whole shoemaker, the whole shirtmaker, the whole automobile manufacturer. Only the many operations occurring co-ordinately together in place and succeeding each other in time can bring to completion shirt, shoes, or whatever else the factory may be producing.

And for the product, the operations have no personal import. It does not matter *who* performs them. The operators serve as impersonally as any replaceable machine part. They need know nothing about the materials they are working on: where they came from, what had been done to them before they reached the factory, how they had been brought, by whom, at what cost, and so on. Nor need they know any of these things about the machines they work at and the other stuffs and tools they use. So long as they perform their assigned operations precisely and in the predetermined order, the product will result. They do know that someone must sell it and someone must buy it and use it if they themselves are to receive wages, but they neither care, nor can know, who. The distributor and the consumer are as impersonal, as anonymous, as the producer.

Our industrial economy makes producer, distributor, consumer interdependent, but the interdependence is blind and unaware, imposed from without, not perceived, understood, and consciously realized from within. Minus such insight and realization, the interdependence of the factory operatives is like that of the parts of a clock or any other interlocking mechanism; their role is to be gadgets of a machine, not members of a community.

Transposition from the level of a machine-part to the level of a member of a community is often accomplished by means of a trade-union. As a "craft-union" this is an association of individuals who, earning their livings by working at the same vocation, pool their interests primarily as competitors for wages against operatives in different fields and against man-

agements and owners in their own; and secondarily, as competitors in the skills and knowledge of their craft. They constitute themselves a society by their agreement on aims, means,
methods for their union. Those terms of union combine the
workmen's diverse personalities into this social unity. Initially,
the unity of the union is predicated on a conflict with others,
on a common struggle with a common foe, corporate or individual: on a fight to make sure that the labors by which the
members earn their livings will be consummated by a wage
envelope on whose content they may rely the better to live
their lives. That wage envelope is the *conditio sine qua non* of
how, and how well, they live their lives.

Now, in the commonsense of these "gainfully employed"
individuals it is the spending of what they earn, not the earning
of what they spend, that is postulated as the experience of culture. Their commonsense opposes culture to vocation. The
prejudices or principles of the "cultured classes" exalt and
consecrate that antithesis, and enshrine it in the conception of
the "liberal education," traditionally interpreted as the education
befitting a free man, which shapes him into a being of "culture
and refinement." This commonsense and this tradition assimilate vocation to labor and culture to leisure. And since most
people work by day and are at leisure by night, vocation tends
to take up the whole of their day life, and culture to constitute
their night life, if they have one. We should, of course, comprehend in night life all the wakeful periods—sabbaths, holi-
days, vacations—that are not taken up in earning a living.
Laboring at their vocations by day for a wage or a salary,
people spend their earnings at their leisure by night. Their
daytime role is that of producers; their nighttime role is that
of consumers. And what they consume composes their culture to them. In the succession of day and night, work and
rest, labor and leisure, their day life is a means to their night
life; their labor is a servile necessity and their leisure a free
condition, both as active and as passive. These sequences signalize culture as the ultimate consumer of whatever vocation
produces. Modern man's night life is consummatory. He en-
joys the experiences of this time of day for what they are, as
they are. He does not knowingly take them as he takes his
job or his money, for a means to anything else. Nor does he

crave to exchange them for anything else. His consummatory acquiescence in them signalizes them as his culture.

The stuffs and forms of this culture are, of course, various and varying. Think of what we spend our earnings on, even what we must spend them on, as well as what we want to spend them on. The obviously necessary things are food, clothing, shelter, healing when ill; the less obvious—and if necessary, necessary from habit and not to instinct—are tobacco, liquor, other chemical anodynes, sports, decorations, music, books, plays, pictures, carvings, ceremonies and rites whether religious or secular, and all the other expressions of our humanity. Now when anybody exchanges money earned by day for whatever one of these goods or services, in order to use and consume it by night, he is receiving the end product of some other body's labors of the day. He is buying an embodiment or expression of that other body's knowledge and skill wherewith the latter earns the wage which he in his turn exchanges for others' products to use and consume. In truth, the quality and pattern of any man's culture are here the product of other men's vocations. The distinction here between culture and vocation is diversely functional, not unically substantive.

We need but review the day and the night of any member of a modern community: farmer, urban, suburban. He rises with the sun, or when his factory whistle blows or his alarm clock rings. He is not likely to stop to bathe or shave, or to take a leisurely breakfast with friends or wife and children, read his newspaper or listen to his radio. Rather, he will hurry his morning toilet, don the clothes that go with his occupation, bolt his eggs, gulp his coffee and hurry to whatever vehicle takes him wherever he works—office, or field, or factory or mine and so on. At his place of work he will punch a time clock or by some other provided means register his arrival. Then, until the noon whistle blows, he will be repeating the actions wherewith he earns his living—so many times an hour, hour after hour. The knowledge and know-how which these actions incarnate, if they are not already so, will tend to become automatic and unaware, habitual responses, not conscious perceptions alert to the changing formations that his field and program of action involve. The more "efficient" he becomes, the less aware he is likely to be of the ideo-motor patterns which constitute his efficiency and of the compenetrated memories which this efficiency embodies. His consciousness turns toward quite other interests—objects and actions of his heart's desire or his heart's aversion; the looks and leanings of his "girl-friend," a game of cards or bowls, an ailment he suffers or a state of well-being he cherishes or seeks, a tune he has heard, a movie he has seen, a book he has read, a meal he plans to enjoy, and so forth, diversely. He goes on doing whatever he does to earn his living by, but he does it almost without knowing.

Alongside of his automatic working he experiences an alert knowing of whatever it be that he lives his life in. This concurrent consciousness is often called reverie, and sometimes deprecated as "wool-gathering" or "absence of mind." That which he therein experiences is, by contrast to the experiential actuality of his vocation, more often than not a formation of his culture. The reverie, indeed, might be described as a translation from vocation to culture—an escape from his job, and from his on-the-job relations to fellow workers, that earn him his living, to the works of other persons and to his off-the-job relations with still other persons, wherein he lives his life.

The bell or whistle or horn that stops his unthinking operations as producer, also cuts off his inward perceptions as consumer. Reflex and reverie arrest together. The earner wakens to the world around him, with its people and forms and movements changing patterns and directions. As he goes to wash his hands or otherwise ready himself for his midday meal, they turn in his experience from unnoticed conditions to significant presences. Eating lunch, he may pass the time of day with fellow workers—but the talk is not very often about the pace and patterns of his work, nor very long, nor very intent about anything. Lunch-time is a short time: bread and meat and sweet are bolted, drink is gulped, the smoke is snatched. The eating tends to be a restoking of a labor-expending animal engine, renewing its "horse power" with so many calories of fuel which laboring oxidized into fatigue-products. The diet hardly figures as food feeding a human being concerned about its texture, taste and fragrance, how it looks and how it is served.

Those concerns are cultural concerns. They are consummatory. They are contents of culture as end products of diverse modes of processing an identical stuff. They come into the foreground of an earner's experience when the earning leaves off and the spending comes on. Often, the change looks as radical as any change from bondage to freedom. After the signal to stop working is heard, the operative begins a series of self-alterations which may not be completed till after he has reached home. The washing-up is far more comprehensive than at midday, often including shave, bath, an entirely fresh toilet. The work-clothes of the day are replaced by the leisure-clothes of the night, dress or undress as the plans of the night life require. Our earner is a different person, with different attitudes and interests as he now enters upon this life. He does not take dinner for granted, as he takes lunch. He is alert to the what and the where and the how of his dining. If he lives in, or close to, some large city, he can choose the style of his meal —for example, home-cooked, French, Hungarian, German, Armenian, Yiddish, Mexican, Chinese. Each of these styles is the product of an integral kitchen culture: each possesses its own singularities of texture, taste and fragrance, of garniture and service, with each go characteristically decorated settings, characteristic accessories of ornamentation and entertainment. Each is the point of impact and experience of an unperceived unknown, even unsuspected, formation of faiths, works, ways and speech whose communal singularity the words *French, Chinese* and so on, symbolize.

Although some of the raw material used in cooking is special to a specific kitchen—like bird's-nest soup in Chinese cooking —most of it is identical and standard: fish and fowl, meats and game, fruits and grains and vegetables such as mankind feed on, everywhere in the world. The difference between one kitchen culture and another is not in what is cooked, but in *how* it is cooked; not in the calories and vitamins that compose it, but in the recipes according to which they are transformed from raw materials into nourishing gratifications of the palate, pleasures of the eye, and satisfactions of the stomach. These recipes record a traditional knowledge and skill which each generation of cooks learns and passes on to the next. Cooking is not merely an assuaging of hunger. Cooking is the art of producing for the eye ever varied configurations and for the palate ever greater harmonic diversifications of tastes and textures and fragrances out of identical substances. Cooking is a basic vocation of man.

But we rarely think of cooking as a component of culture, to say nothing of thinking it as a primal component. Nor, since before Aristotle, have we been disposed to appraise cooks as culture-bearers. To merit this eulogium they would have to function not only as producers of meals but as sensitive and discriminating consumers of meals. One word for such consumers is *gourmet*. In the French of its origin this word first denoted a person who earned his living by tasting wines and discriminating their flavor and bouquet. Wine-tasting, like tea-tasting, is still a vocation learned through the cultivation and refinement of the sensitivities of nose, tongue and palate, the organs wherewith we savor and appraise wines and teas among other things. But the producers answering to this vocation are not therefore recognized as men of culture and refinement, nor are they any longer called gourmets. We call gourmets the men and women whose sensitivities of nose, tongue and palate serve them as organs of consumption. They are connoisseurs of tastes, textures, bouquets and substances. For their opposites, usage has the word, *gourmand*, the glutton who gulps and gormandizes and cares not a hang for the look, savor or scent of the stuff he bolts; factory hands at lunch might be called *gourmands*. The gourmet is also called "epicure," and that word brings the connotation of the Athenian sage, Epicurus, and of his teachings concerning nature and man, man's destiny and the conduct of his life. This teaching is a philosophic faith. Wherever such an overall faith, with its conspectus of ends and means, groups and goals is actually in play, there accrues to the word "culture" depth and span that diversify its conventional meaning.

In our history, the case has been the opposite with "epicure" and "gourmet." The words signalize only the expertise of the senses of touch, taste and smell, disciplined to the pursuit, and fitted to the enjoyment, of these experiences. The preparers of those enjoyments Shakespeare speaks of in *Antony and Cleo-*

patra, I think, as epicurean cooks, who sharpen with cloyless sauce Antony's appetite. Although it is the sauce, far more than the substance, that serves the gourmet's epicuric appetite, his concentration on it is religiously exclusive and devout. A dinner of gourmets is purely a dinner, like a priestly ceremonial fixed in its rites and performed duly and in order. Nothing extrinsic to savoring and smelling, chewing and swallowing, is admitted to profane the sacred event—no music, no conversation on alien themes, no distracting thoughts or sights or sounds, such as supplement the menus of unepicuric diners.

To the latter the dinner of his night life is a liberation from the furnace stoking of his day life; the dining room, the table, the tableware, the linen, the decorations, the companions, the conversation, the music, dancing too, perhaps—all the diverse thoughts and sights and sounds—supplement and transfigure the manifold looks and savors and scents of the comestibles, joining with them into a self-orchestrating composition wherein the uses of each part may be enhanced by the harmonic feel of its vital interplay with all the others. It is the ongoing orchestration which exercises the liberating function. In this function one of our meanings of culture lives and moves and has its being.

When our diners rise from their table, their night life still flowers variously through their waking hours. It may bud and bourgeon via theater, opera, a concert, a lecture, art galleries, museums, radio or television, baseball, boxing, wrestling, necking, cards, pool, bowling, the practice or contemplation of one or another form of sport, gaming, instruction, entertainment, "creative" or recreational. Even the mattress one lies on and the bed one sleeps in may have come to stand in consciousness as the nexus of a configuration of images and ideas, symbols and implications—recall such an advertiser's solicitation with pictures of beauties beautifully asleep on form-fitting mattresses, with words such as "beautyrest"—which translate going to sleep and waking up into cultural experiences.

II

Of course what I have up to now set down signalizes the limit which an indefinitely varying variable might reach, and sometimes does. It is enough to establish the observation that we earn by day, working, and spend by night, living; that we live *by* our vocations and live *in* our cultures; but also that the traditional distinction between vocation and culture is not essential but contingent.

True, the distinction is found in simple societies whose cooks, farmers, weavers and otherwise workers are almost exclusively co-operative women; whose hunters, warriors, gamesmen and otherwise exhibitors of prowess are almost exclusively competitive men. But as occupations diversify, more and more the male joins the female of the species in the upkeep and growth of the changing economy; arts and crafts, with their attendant rituals and rotes become vocations of the males, workmanship replaces exploit as the demonstration of personal worth, and the arts of speech and song are joined to visual and manual arts, to point up present achievement, recall past performance, and inspire future undertaking. Each vocation is the spring of a culture that it generates and nourishes, perhaps as a bird generates and nourishes its plumage and projects its songs, or as a plant grows its leaves and blooms and releases its fruit and seed. They come to eye or ear, nose or mouth, as consequences, not causes, and as consequences that, like cut flowers, do not long survive apart from their causes. In the configurations of culture and vocation, the enduring operative causes are distinguishable as relations of men, women and children to one another, and to the scenes of their struggles to live and not die, to progress and not regress.

The simplest relationships anyone takes on are, of course, familial. There is always a mother, and almost always a father. The three or two-member family is the smallest, simplest society so far distinguished. But its inner relations may be variously manifold and complex. Love and hate, dependence and rebellion, submission and defiance or evasion, competition and emulation or co-operation and support may compound into polymorphous sentiments whose dominant direction only expression by symbol or action discloses. The boundaries which define such expression are set by the acting individual's perception of the import for his own survival of his scene and of its *dramatis personae*. Much that tradition calls culture consists in formations of such boundaries as procedures in thinking, feeding, loving, fighting, playing, working—communing with men, animals and gods, through the media of signs, symbols, speech and icons that preserve as well as utter and denote the procedures.

Thus, culturally, a family may be anything but simple. The network of relationships that a child takes on with birth diversifies in weave and span as it grows up. Growing up is entering into a progressive diversification of relationships. Words such as brothers, sisters, uncles, aunts, cousins, grandparents, pupils, schoolmates, playmates, teammates, fellow worker, church member, party member, union member, soldier, voter, lover, husband, and so on without end, denote modes of association of individual with individual. The form and function of each such association is different from every other; each relates its members to one another in terms of its own singularity of form and function. Each in so doing shuts out and cuts off other configurations of goings and goals. Its purpose and program constitute it an individuality on its own account with its identifying principles and practices that generate, as it goes on struggling to go on struggling, its characteristic works, ways, speech, imageries and memories.

Among free peoples, most such associations are what we call voluntary; they form, change, grow, dissolve, at the option of the individuals who constitute them, are creations of their consent. Each such individual decides for himself, on impulse or according to reason as he chooses, to join this society or leave that. His belonging or not is an inner commitment expressed by a pattern of outer behavior. Even his relation to his family, which he is born into by no known choice of his own, is a function of this commitment, for he can reënforce "accident of birth" by consent and loyalty or nullify it by withdrawal from all association with the members of the family and the refusal of all family responsibility. Such inner rejection and nonparticipation is much more widespread than is realized. It serves the individual who is shut into an authoritarian society as a pervasive insurance of his personal integrity and freedom, to which he gives outward manifestation by means of lag, inefficiency and sabotage; in the army, a traditionally authoritarian society, this is called "soldiering"; it is a part of "the army way" and intrinsic to military culture. It underlies the *ahimsa* which Gandhi employed as an instrument of "non-violent" warfare against the British *raj* in India. Societies which carry a tradition of freedom seem to have no other word or other token for nonparticipation and inner withdrawal as a characteristic of the group-culture. Of course these attitudes occur and may on occasion become pervasive. But they do not become constitutive, they do not become traditional. That is, they become neither the differentiating traits of a society's present, nor carriers of a pattern, diversely repeating itself yet altering, in a group's life history. Life history is the stuff of which tradition makes itself. That word means, literally, a carrying on, a continuous ongoing—but a carrying on, or ongoing, as any person's life goes on, not changelessly, but as a process of changing, where the old phases both continue in the new and are altered by the new. Self-preservation, whether of an individual or a group, is this process wherein the past endures only as it lives on in the present and future, and lives on only as it is changed by them.

In this respect, a group-life prolongs and redirects the lives of the individuals whose association generates, sustains and impels the formations of the group. Individuals not only live and move and nourish their being amid traditions, they are themselves traditions. That is, as animal organisms, as sources, they are configurations of action-patterns on gradients and with goals implicit in their genes, in their inheritance, and diversely explicated *via* the transactions or give-and-take with the surroundings wherein they work, fight and worry to live and to grow. Those words name ideo-motor formations of commitment and withdrawal, the creative impulsions that propel individual characters in one direction when their associations are authoritarian, in a diversity of others when free.

In freedom, commitment and withdrawal are collaborative decisions of the individual, not compulsions of his group or of any of its institutions. He decides as desire prompts and reason perceives. Thence we call his relationships with others voluntary; the "social mobility" of free societies is a function of them and obtains as the *élan* of the individual's personal history. To the observer, this mobility is the behavior of a living body. Its freedom would be but a blind freedom unless it were also signalizing a mobility of intent, feeling and intellection whose confluences make up the stream of consciousness whereof, first and last, the tradition consists which we call the psyche of that soma. The individual, always indivisibly psyche and soma, is his personal history in the making. *His* personal history and no other. He is a unique psychosomatic tradition. His present is a flowing of a singular past into a singular future that in joining, alters the past whose future it becomes.

III

The dogma that we cannot change the past is not an understanding of the process of change but a prejudice of our resistance to it and a static illusion symbolizing our fear of it. What else is there to change? What else is the present but the past changing? What else is the past but the old substance or energy which the new future suffuses and reshapes precisely because the innovations which characterize future *as* future have nowhere else to arise or to be? Because, hence, all quanta of past and future are in such wise experienced together—as a process of self-location of changes within the sames which they change from—that the changes are perceived as a self-altering identity, or the identity as a self-unifying diversification. This is what the all-pervasive "sense of time" perceives; what our attention discriminates as present, past and future.

Philosophic reasoning long, long ago repudiated the perception as violating all logic, too irrational to be anything but truth's opposite, Maya, unreliable illusion, which would make him who relies on it to perish. During millennia generations of philosophers East and West have sustained this line of reasoning, diversifying its forms without impairing its intent. But within the past century philosophic thinking on this theme has developed signal innovations. Discourse, in the context of the new biology and the new physics, has taken a radically new turn, establishing the reality of this irrational, alogical confluence of past and future, sameness and change, continuation and mutation, which make up the flux of time, establishing the validity of Maya and the truth of appearance. Pioneers of the new turn have been, each with his own direction and quality of vision and of expression, William James, Alfred North Whitehead, Henri Bergson, Canning Schiller, John Dewey. New words have come into use to signalize the new insights— "real duration," "flux," "process," "temporalism," "functionalism." New views of what is man and what is culture have come into play. Most sciences of man now endeavor to get close to the perceptual presence of the human condition. Most now recognize that a person alike as soul and as body is a living past, a dynamic pattern of memories we call according to their span, instincts, habits, attitudes, images, concepts—symbolized by words and signs—which form and reform, as he grows up and grows old, into the personal history that his struggle to go on struggling creates.

And as the person, so the groups which group him or with which he groups himself. Even those we regard as self-repeating, without alteration, alter. But some may be altering as a tree grows, with the life pressing from the center of origin to the outermost edge, leaving behind a dead pith, and ring after ring of matter devoid of sense and movement; alive, responsive, growing, only at a thin frontier of sensibility and action, which thrusts against boundaries under a protective bark. The tradition of such societies—their faiths, their ways, their works —may go on changing as slowly as a glacier moves, crumbling down, crumbling down like Vachel Lindsay's Empire of China, and building up, building up like any growing plant. That of others may be as kinetic at the pith as under the bark, and be exercising vital functions through its entire order of rings.

Drag or push and pull, each society is, for the individuals in whose lives it lives, a patterned environment. Its formations so work as to strengthen and enlarge, or to weaken and contract, his personal singularity. His safety is their numbers; his freedom—as a social process, not a psychosomatic quality—is their diversity. The more of them he can join or leave, the more varied their forms and functions, the more abundant, the freer, the richer, the more civilized, is likely to be the personality which lives and moves and nourishes its being among the diverse communions. It is the variety and range of his participations which does in fact distinguish a civilized man from an uncivilized, a man of faith and reason from an unreasoning fanatic, a democrat from a totalitarian, a man of culture from a barbarian. Such a man obviously orchestrates a growing pluralism of associations into the wholeness of his individuality.

IV

The distinction just denoted is not one that we readily accept to live by. We suffer an animal insecurity before whatever differs from the selves of heritage and habit we struggle to "preserve." The different evokes at least uneasiness which may mount to anxiety, to fear, to rage. We have to learn to acquiesce in change for our own faiths and works and to overcome our disposition to appraise such change in others as breach of faith and deficiency of character save when it confronts our own diversifications with no challenge, but surely confirms our views and values by conforming to them. That we should have to respect the different, should have to labor to understand and appreciate it, should have to orchestrate our own felt uniqueness with a singularity not less but even more demanding, comes upon us as a compulsion which we instinctively would avert from. Sometimes we protect ourselves by ostracizing that different, sometimes by coercing, indenturing or enslaving it, sometimes by liquidating it. Always we would, if we could, digest it culturally as we digest vegetables and animals biologically. The propensity is to "assimilate" the culturally diverse, converting the differences into sameness with one's own culture, while what cannot be so converted because one is too weak or another is too strong, tends to be excreted, isolated, destroyed, as an offense, an unworthiness, a foe of the good, the true and the beautiful.

Either way, mankind are disposed to make an end of those other cultural identities as they make an end of the plants and animals which they take for food-supply, causing them to die that they themselves may not die. Under certain conditions, this disposition may become a ruling passion, the impulsion of a program whose utterance by rite and rote is articulated into a creed and a code respecting human nature, human destiny and human relations. The articulation becomes a community's dominant ideal, its ethos and its spirit. The resulting psychosomatic images tend to drive from consciousness the ineluctable perception that not only do we require perennial replenishment of the nourishing animals and plants we cause to die in order that we may ourselves not die, but that other cultures must likewise go on living and producing abundantly if our own is also to live and not die. In recent history, such suppressive images have dominated Germany and Russia, Spain and the other lands where Roman sacerdotalism holds a religious monopoly. They are ancestral in Islam and insurgent in Israel. An imperialism of the mind is projected, and a cultural colonialism set up, both postulated on power to impose on the diverse conformation or servitude. Diversities in the languages, religions, the arts, the sciences, are hunted down, persecuted and penalized. The entire psychosomatic economy —from agriculture and animal husbandry to the expressive culture of ideas and the paideia of men—is required to feed on itself and to grow by what it feeds on. If successful, the result is that, save for the bootlegging of domestic diversifications and the smuggling of foreign diversities, starvation and sterility become destiny for body and soul alike.

But on the whole and in the long run such imperialisms win only battles, not wars. No institution of any civilization ever gathers enough power to impose an everlasting submission and servitude upon the different, or to suppress differentiation within the same. Every authoritarian culture, hence, has its perennial spyings and inquisitions and purgings, and every non-authoritarian culture seeks them on occasion, witness mccarthyism in mid-century United States.

Broadly, cultural history draws upon a global intercultural war of all against all, every so often relaxing into a sort of balance of cultural power, and on occasion coming to agreements, acquiescing in the diversifications and diversities which are the stuff of experience, replacing dominance over difference with equal rights for the different and with free trade between differences in thoughts and services and things.

This pattern of interpersonal and intergroup communication is the one which the arts and sciences have always followed when they were free, and seek when they are not free. It is the pattern which the United Nations Educational, Scientific and Cultural Organization endeavors to embody and the United Nations Organization pretends to. It would comprehend some two and one-half billion men, women and children, diversely united into thousands upon thousands of diverse cultural groups within which they are being born, growing up, growing old, dying, in a struggle to go on struggling thus and so and not otherwise, which we call self-preservation. The patterns range from the manifold communities of the Arctic Circle Eskimos, Australian blackfellows or African Negroes, to American redskins or Euro-American whiteskins. They range from families and clans and tribes and guilds and gangs and friendly societies, to clubs and cities and counties and nations and alliances of nations. They span associations combined with associations, all coming down finally to the basic unit of combination—the person with his individual history. Each such unit lives an individual different from the others. Each must needs dwell or work or play or fight with others near him who are his face-to-face associates. Each is linked to still others with whom his conscious bonds are symbolic and imaginative, and his practical bonds unperceived operations and processes, mediated by events which move in set sequences from them to him.

V

Of the linkages, the most pervasive and important is, of course, language. Language—its phonetic substance, its intrinsic patterns as vehicles of meanings, its modes of change and all that is intended by the term "usage"—functions both as a shaper and sustainer of a culture; embodies indeed its traditions regarding the human enterprise in the modes that the group whose language it is images the enterprise and transmits the image from generation to generation. There are thousands of languages and dialects, each with its own tradition of usage, its changing phonations and signs and symbols that the dictionaries never catch up with, no matter how often they are revised. The agencies of such change are again many and by no means commensurable. For example, whence come distinctions between "cultured" and uncultured speech, good use and bad in the American language of our time? What are their sanctions? A "400" bored with the correct forms of their class and seeking relief in expressions drawn from the stage, the baseball diamond, the race track, the business office, the dancehall and the bar? A housewife going about her daily round with her heart attuned to the speech of the radio performer of soap opera? Un-American investigations of ambiguously literate congressional committees? Other voices, thespian, sacerdotal, political, journalistic? A will to be "as good as their betters" expressing itself in linguistic emulation of the linguistic Joneses, somewhat in the same manner as the country emulates city fashions in clothes, or as the shops where the poor buy, offer styles first shown by the shops whose customers are the rich?

Another multitude of linkages is designated by the word "religion," and the commonest word in the languages of religion is the word "God." This word is just now more than usually in the mouths of Americans, lay and clerical, and of politicians, lay and professional, from the White House to the back room of the political club, and only God knows what those who are using the word mean by it. Certainly, the meanings received from the theologians of the diverse communions, cults, sects, denominations, factions, that compose the religions of the world's different cultures, are each individual, singular, not to be reduced to a de-individualized One, always and everywhere the same. To find some common, overall meaning, we must needs look away from the concepts and images of whatever God "is," in the sentiment of any one of those religious societies, to what they expect their God to do, and how they expect it to be done. When we inspect the latter, when we turn from a divine "nature" to the divine functions, we find that they are: generally, to remove some presen. hurt or burden, to provide some future health and easement, to save from evil, to save for good. Functionally, "God" means insurance against present danger and future uncertainty when other agencies of insurance are felt to be no longer reliable. The word engenders in the true believer a psychosomatic lift and confidence such as Mr. Aldous Huxley says he experienced when he took mescalin. We experience confidence and lift under a great variety of circumstances, but the commonest linguistic circumstance seems to be the word "God"—a sound and spelling that in the United States signalize some two hundred and fifty American denominations, sects and cults. These two hundred and fifty are but an ambiguous fraction of some seventeen hundred individual divinities, each diverse in that, whatever be the God's "nature," there is an association of men, women and children who put their trust in it to save them from evil and to save them for good. Beside the Crucified One of the Christians there are some sixteen others also Saviors because they have been somehow "crucified." All Gods are members of a variety of pantheons instituted by the companions of the diverse faiths according to the function which the member-gods are designed to exercise; and the whole is at last crystallized in a creed and defined by a code of man-and-god relations. Because of the disposition to appraise whatever is different as therefore dangerous, false and wrong, the religions of the world seem to persevere in a state of war with one another, each denying the other's power to insure against fate and fortune, and seeking to displace the others in the exercising of this function.

Among the items God diversely insures is, of course, the procurement and preparation of food. The gods participate both centrally and tangently in how we provide, prepare, and consume what we eat and drink. And eating and drinking, no less than being born and dying, mating and fighting and building, are, in every society, formations of the struggle to live and to grow in which the gods are held to play powerful roles. The diversities in dress, diet, housing, decoration, ornamentation, cosmetics, first accompany, then go independently of the diversity of divinities and worships. Large or small, the simpler a society, the more homogeneous, the more interdependent and compenetrated are its institutions and beliefs. The more diversified and complex a society, the more mobile are its members, the more loose and external are the relations between them. Its unity tends to be sustained by voluntary commitment to union, and to consist in an ongoing self-orchestration of individuals, each of whom images himself as a self-conscious, choosing, deciding self-directing personality.

VI

This personality-image is a self-incarnating ideal rather than an observed fact. We make it up, in all of its aspects, as we make up our toilet before our mirrors. It is the self that we truly struggle to preserve, and that we perceive only as we create and embody it day by day. It is the standard of our personal being that we work and fight to measure up to, and that we define, shape, nourish and refine by means of what we read and hear and otherwise experience as formations of force, freedom and fulfillment. Their primal material may be today's conspicuous figures of business, state, church, stage, screen or sport, at home or abroad, as we perceive them "in person" or learn of them by hearsay, spoken or printed. They may be familial ancestors, or historic leaders, or heroes of fiction. But their vital meaning, for us, is not their objective presence, but their function in the formation and sustenance of our image of ourselves as we crave to be. They are the culture of this image. Their ideo-motor patterns are the ways upon which we would go. They are our present anticipation of the future we would keep making both as a living and a life. Our attitude toward the image into which we compenetrate them is an act of faith. It is a prophecy about our own future on which we bet our lives. In so far as we act we so channel our energies as to work present faith over into future fact, betting our future on what we believe now. The more that which we believe in now looks back to events we had before experienced, the more we now hope and pray that we experience them soon again (perhaps more intensely and abundantly), the more certain we feel, the more disposed we are to regard our bet as a bet on a sure thing. Repetition being the ground of prediction thus makes for sentiments of continuity and safety; variation, for feelings of insecurity and doubt. What we most ask from science, as from religion, or for that matter, from all the institutions of our society, is a providence to shape our ends by, a foreknowledge by whose light we can determine our foreordinations for ourselves.

In the nature of things, repetitions are collective, variations are individual. The science and arts of hunting, seeding and growing foodstuffs and of preparing them for consumption; the knowledge and know-how of devising tools and weapons and utensils, of producing shelter and clothing, of identifying and fighting disease and other enemies, human and nonhuman, are repeated, generation to generation, as configurations of customs, folkways, mysteries of guild and craft. The configurations combine into a group-personality whose image the group's mores project and define as a creed wherein the older generation indoctrinates the younger, and a code whereunder the older so disciplines the younger as to mold it, like Jehovah God, into an image of itself. Each group, every generation of it, intends and cultivates a different, and diversifying image, each exemplifies a different and diversifying group-personality. For this we may take the word "culture" as a synonym.

So, the members of any and all such groups, having expressed their united ways and works in spoken and graphic signs, images and symbols, become through and in them conscious of themselves as units of a collective being, possessed of an ethos or spirit or culture other than their simple togetherness. They come to see themselves as a chosen people and to distinguish their ethos from others' as ineffably, uniquely precious. "We," its spokesmen will then proclaim, "are alone the right ones, the true, the good, the beautiful ones. What is unlike us is by nature inferior to us and destined to obey and serve us or perish." The history of culture records one instance after another of such invidious cultural self-consciousness. The Greeks segregated mankind into Hellenes and barbarians, and their segregation has its puerile transposition in the self-segregation of the Greek-letter fraternities from the literate "barbs" of American colleges. The barbarians were all who were not Greeks, couldn't speak the Greek language and were unhabituated in Greek ways—alone the right ways. We continue to use the word "barbarian" in this sense. Anybody is a barbarian whose manners and morals and standards differ from ours. Or if not a barbarian, such a body is "vulgar" or "foreign" or "Democrat" or "Dixiecrat" or "Republican" as the case may be. Whatever the symbol, it is the signature of an inferior status. And if the users should themselves feel inferior, for whatever reason, they insist the more fiercely on the inferiority of others, much as people afraid whistle in the dark.

The Jews' equivalent for the Greeks' "barbarian" was "gentile"—the people unchosen, set in contrast to the Lord's Chosen People. When Christianism differentiated from a cult into a culture, "Christian" replaced "Jew" as the synonym for "chosen," elect unto salvation, and Jew, pagan, infidel, misbeliever, became diverse terms for "reject," condemned unto destruction. Mohammedan cultures project a similar division and segregation, so does Brahminism, with its prescriptions and taboos to ward off contamination from all beings not Brahmin, especially Untouchables, whose mere existence is defilement. Nor is our own country, with an ethos inimical to the practice, free of it. Our traditional isolationism, our laws respecting immigration and our use of the epithets "alien," "foreign," our image of the "100 per cent American," our "Daughters of the American Revolution," unheeding of the ideals the Revolution was fought for, their brothers, the Sons; the Ku Klux Klan, all are groups with a creed and code, invidiously setting apart themselves, the elect, from the rest of the nation, somehow the reject. Hitler, again, segregated mankind into two races—the Chosen Nazi race and the rejected human race, destined to pursue a mean existence as the servile Yahoos of the Nazi elect. The Communist variant of the segregative aggression sets over against "bourgeois" mankind elect "people's democracies" or "workers' republics," or "proletarian dictatorships" entitled to rank, privilege, and status that no noncommunist may challenge or deny and every noncommunist must believe, obey and serve.

The practice, it may be seen, is universal and endemic. No society, no culture, is exempt from it. Nor is any individual. It is one form of a spontaneous recoil from, and aggression against, the different. Its consequences in interpersonal and intergroup relations are denoted by such words as conquest, subordination, exploitation, enslavement, assimilation, destruction and their contraries. The choices any member of a group lives by tend to be only those which arise within the boundaries of his group, and to be limited by their congruity with his commitment to that whole, be it religious, occupational, linguistic, political, or whatever. Whoso does not share the commitment, whoso is not one of the In-group it circumscribes, is then penalized simply for not being *in*. The members of an In-group tend to maintain it as a closed self-repeating static society, allergic to all variation and change.

VII

On the record, the tendency projects a purpose, not an achievement, a desire or claim, not a fact. There are no closed or static societies. All change, in and by their struggles not to change, quite like the individuals who are their life-force. So-called closed societies, such as, for example, Sparta, the Jewries, the Roman Church, the Hitlerites, the Stalinites, the Ku Klux Klan strive or strove to achieve, are disclosed as societies where the power-holders endeavor to inhibit differentiation from without. Penalties upon the stranger and sojourner, censorships, tariffs, iron curtains, secret police, and other devices to arrest free communication are their instruments of policy. That, on the whole and in the long run, this is a self-defeating policy, has never prevented demagogic tyrants or dictators from proposing it; or, when and if they took power, from launching it, and even for a time successfully prosecuting it.

In the nature of things such success does not endure. The power of a cultural economy to impose its creeds and codes and install its works and ways fails because its ethos sickens and its institutions loosen and come apart; or because it suffers defeat at the hands of another culture whose diversity it has treated as an adversity. When this happens, pretension replaces power; the values of the ethos are declared to be purely spiritual values; their paramountcy is declared independent of all coercive force; they are portrayed as an unmoved mover drawing by its goodness all that differs into conformation with itself. Thus when Athens had suffered total defeat at the hands of Sparta, when thereafter the Macedonians had demonstrated that they were the force preponderant over the Hellenes, many Athenians ceased to image their *polis* as a politico-military domination and came to envisage it as a liberating culture. The patriot rhetorician, Isocrates, a contemporary of Aristotle —who was the tutor, be it remembered, of Alexander of Macedon and the "Philosophus" of Thomas Aquinas—in an oration, *Panegyricus,* voiced this transvaluation of his *polis:* "Athens has brought it about that the name Hellene no longer suggests a race but an intelligence, and that the title, Hellene, is applied rather to those who share our culture than to those who share a common blood." Alexander shared the culture to the point that his armies fought the battles of a missionary cultural imperialism that carried the Hellenic paideia to Egypt, Judea, the riverlands of Arabia, up to the Khotan. Whether the Hellenic idea could of itself have effected the Hellenistic conversion of the Middle East with no sanctions of physical force, is an open question to which the Hellenization of the Romans by the Greeks they conquered suggests an inconclusive affirmative in answer.

But this is another story. The high point of the one we are considering is the detachment of culture from race and soil, its equation to an "intelligence," a system of attitudes, thoughts and things, capable of itself to shape anyone's experience anywhere. A similar detachment was envisaged by the Jews during the exile, when the Hebraism of the Dispersed was first reshaped toward the Judaism of the Ingathered. But the record of millennia does not show that Judaism came to be thought as an independent spirit, the same everywhere on the globe. Until the democratic revolution its creed and code continued to nourish the sentiment of blood and soil as the focal point for true Judaism, and much of the travail and tragedy of Jewish history, and much of what is singular to Jewish culture derives from its credo regarding Exile and Return, rendering the images and discourse regarding Return the culture of the exile.

This diverse development, Hellenic and Hebraic, converged toward a common consequence. Other, in all likelihood even more intimate and potent, forces worked toward the same consequence. This is the persisting segregation of culture from vocation, psyche from soma, form from matter. The tradition of thinking them dualistically maintains so great a momentum that it still overrides all different notions. We still postulate two economies, an economy of vocation and an economy of culture and bet our daily lives on this postulate; working to earn our livings, and spending what we earn to live our lives, all too often experiencing the latter as release and salvation from the former, and nothing else besides.

We must note, however, that the tradition draws upon a dualism still earlier than that which came with the liberation of a people's ethos—signalized by its language, its productions in letters, in the graphic and plastic arts, in cultus, and in science—from the people that produced it and the land where it was produced. The liberation is here equivalent to mobility, and is a consequence of the independence of the completed product from the processes which have produced it, so that it may go upon the winds of trade and talk while producer and process continue where they were. Culture thus gets assimilated to product, vocation to production, culture to leisure, vocation to labor, culture to end, vocation to instrument. So again culture becomes the consumption of the product, vocation the production of whatever is consumed. Culture becomes the vocation of persons who are free to live without working, vocation the life of persons who must work without living.

In the ethos of the Greek *polis*, this antithesis shaped the entire economy. It appraised labor and production as mean and servile, leisure and consumption as noble and free. Aristotle speaks of the slave as a tool with life in it, of the tool as a lifeless slave. He looks upon people who work with their hands as incapable of the dignity and worth proper to a free man, by nature unable to perceive the truth of things because unable to participate in the consummatory delights of a well-prepared meal, of well-played music, of aptly reasoned ideas. Not the cook knows the truth of food, nor the player the inwardness of music, nor the poet or actor, inspired as they may be, the discourse of reason. The consumer, whose consumption is the end, who tastes, smells, savors, discriminates, listens and judges, the products of these producers, he knows the truth of them; and it is by his critical diversified and diversifying perceptions, discriminations, judgments, decisions, that their production is warranted or condemned. It is these perceptions that constitute the paideia of the generations, that are the stuff of education, and the matter and method wherewith the new generations are disciplined into freedom and equipped with the knowledge and skills worthy of the free man. To be thus free was to be free from the labor without which this freedom cannot obtain. It meant the right of power to reap what another sowed, to use what another made and to have the sowers and makers always at one's command. Paideia rested on a slave economy; wherein labor has no dignity and the insights and skills of the producer are not liberal arts but servile disciplines degrading to the free.

This outlawing of labor from liberty, this cutting leisure off from production, which the "ages of faith" transposed into the subordination of the *vita activa* to the *vita contemplativa*, received dogmatic confirmation from the Christian reworking of the Eden story of the Old Testament. By force of this reworking, labor is a curse laid by God upon the whole breed of Adam as punishment for Adam's disobedience of the divine commandment not to eat of the fruit of the tree of knowledge of good and evil lest he die. Because Eve and Adam did eat of this fruit, Jehovah God cursed them: "Unto the woman he said, I will greatly multiply thy pain and thy conception: in pain thou shalt bring forth children; and thy desire shall be to thy husband, and he shall rule over thee. And unto Adam he said, Because thou hast hearkened unto the voice of thy wife, and hast eaten of the tree, of which I commanded thee, saying: *Thou shalt not eat of it:* cursed is the ground for thy sake; in toil shalt thou eat of it all the days of thy life: thorns also and thistles shall it bring forth to thee; and thou shalt eat of the herb of the fields; in the sweat of thy face shalt thou eat bread until thou return unto ground, for out of it thou wast taken; for dust thou art and unto dust thou shalt return." And Jehovah God drove out that first man from the bounteous Garden of Eden, where he had lived in leisured immortality, now in mortality "to till the ground from whence he was taken" and whereto he is now condemned to return.

The fusion of the Hebraic with the Hellenic appraisal of the significance of labor and leisure, wherewith the Christian one starts, became the traditional rationalization of the different status given culture and vocation by our Western world, which still speaks of the "gentleman of culture and refinement" but never similarly qualifies the working man. The gentleman is by definition a person well born—that is, a descendant who collects their images and who has been taught the names and deeds of his ancestors and his ancestors' ancestors; who has been disciplined in the arts of fighting and ruling; whose senses have been taught to discriminate tastes and smells and textures, sights and sounds and movements, images and symbols and to savor and consume them all according to the code of his heritage and station. The personality-image he presumably strives, day in day out, to embody, becomes, like a people's ethos, a coded configuration of attitudes, speech, manners, drink, diet, sports and other accomplishments. These, signalized by words, images and other symbols are used for gradations of individual self-realization that any reader can then take to himself and emulate—even getting drunk may call for doing so like a lord, or carrying one's liquor like a gent. It provides the image of the Jones of culture and refinement with whom the un-Jones hurries to keep up.

Castiglione's *Il Cortegiano* provided such a gradation; so did Peacham's *Compleat Gentleman;* so did Spenser's *Faerie Queen.* So did Moliere's derisive *Bourgeois-Gentilhomme* and Hogarth's *Rake's Progress* and *Good and Idle Apprentice.* With the changing times, changing ethos, the image also changes. But it departs little from the basic dualism of culture and vocation. Whether it is one disclosed by Cardinal Newman's idea of a university, by Matthew Arnold's disquisitions in *Literature and Dogma*, or *Culture and Anarchy*, by Charles W. Eliot's *ad hoc* definition of the gentleman of democracy, by the counter-Arnoldian figure implicit in T. S. Eliot's *Notes on Culture*, the point of no return is the segregation of the codes of the consumption of products from the arts of producing the products consumed.

VIII

Culture, exclusively so taken and pursued, is a cut-flower culture. It is a sensitive plant doomed to fade early and perish even in the most hydroponic gentleman of culture and refinement. For it is a terminal product cut off from its roots as well as its soil, and therefore kept alive by only artificial means. Obviously, the roots and soil can be alone the vocations that the cultures consummate in what Matthew Arnold, borrowing from Jonathan Swift, called "sweetness and light," but likewise, as our own times know, in a no less enlightening bitterness and gloom. Also our own times are aware, as earlier ones were not, that culture cannot be segregated from vocation and live, any more than the "consumption" of the economist can continue independent of "production." It needs no Freud, calling up the arts as anodynes of man from his unconscious' vasty deep, to tell us that they are devices to ease our struggles —with one another and with the nonhuman scene—to go on struggling, and that they serve as liberations from toil, pain and other people. Freud, discontent like Rousseau with the obstacles between ambition and realization that he felt society's ways and values had interposed for him, doubted "whether the amenities of culture are worth the cost of nervous strain imposed on us." Nevertheless, again like Rousseau, he continued an unceasing consumer of those amenities. He was too wise himself to return to the nature of which culture is a humanization, and too understanding not to recognize that, in this humanization, vocation is both the creative and the re-creative force. But, exploring the unremembered past of men and women by bringing it to conscious remembrance, he discerned also that the consummatory consciousness which we are born to live and grow in, has been so segregated from the vocations of modern man, that the labor by which he earns his living becomes by economists' definition patterned effort painfully executed for the sake of the leisure wherein he lives his life. Vocation thus is made a necessary evil, without joy and without vision; culture is made a compensatory contingent anodyne, pause without direction, assuagement without healing, on occasion restorative, never progressive, enlarging, fulfilling.

Other judgments, impelled by very different assumptions, also converge toward Freud's appraisals. Such are those of the American platonizers, Paul More and Irving Babbitt; of the romanist or romanizing Thomists and neo-Thomists among whom spokesmen in America are such contrasted voices as Jacques Maritain and Robert Hutchins. These are variations within, not divergences from, the Judaeo-Hellenisticism of the Christian establishments.

IX

But these are vociferous, not prevalent. More general are appraisals coming soon after various units of the population of Europe took the Democratic Idea for their fighting faith. One such is Giuseppe Mazzini's, who projected a new rationale, giving their manifold struggles for freedom from alien rule a vital center, by identifying it as a struggle for the freedom of the native culture to grow and fulfill itself. Mazzini was an Italian nationalist. But his nationalism was a nationalism of culture, sustaining itself in equal liberty of growth and communication with all other national cultures. He envisaged the national cultures as having each its own singularity of function and form, and as joined together in the international undertakings whose diversities are organic units of the total life that is European civilization. In Mazzini's vision of the national culture, vocation and culture could not be dual. The restoration of pleasure to labor and of the values of consumption to the efforts of production was inherent in the achievement through culture of equal liberty for the unequal.

To authorized spokesmen for the German envisagement of culture this co-operative internationalist nationalism of Mazzini's carried no conviction. Their own creed and code were so incommensurable, so unacceptable to non-Germans, that usage keeps their word for culture untranslated. To the sensibilities of the free world *Kultur* does not mean culture. It means a nineteenth- and twentieth-century representation of an exclusive racism of attitudes, thoughts and things. Its apostles and proponents count romantic philosophers like Johann Gottlieb Fichte, romanticists of letters and the arts like the von Schlegels, like Richard Wagner, propagandists of *Deutschtum* like Houston Stewart Chamberlain, and more ambiguously, Oswald Spengler; apostles of Hitlerism like Alfred Rosenberg and Hitler in person. All these divide mankind, as we have seen, into a creative, Kultur-breeding Nordic or Nazi race, and another, the human race—the former, the consecrated to the authorized liberties of culture, the latter capable only of the predestined servilities of vocation.

The racism of the apostles of Kultur was a counter not alone to the racio-cultural egalitarianism of Mazzini. It was an attack as well upon the new claims for workmen growing in a new way from the Democratic Idea. With the industrial revolution, which made culture more than ever a product of the cities, came an ever-increasing movement of people from farm work to factory work, and an ever-hardening division between the occupations and meanings of the working day and the occupations and meanings of the resting night. This translation of the agricultural laborer into the industrial worker, was perhaps a concomitant of the industrial division of labor, which so divided the production of the product of industrial labor that, as we have already observed, the persons employed in it are cut down from craftsmen responsible for the whole product into operatives responsible for a minute fraction of it. Where the tools of craftsmen are extensions of their own persons, and their products emerge bearing the signature of their singularities, the tools of operatives are stationary machines with mobile parts, which the operatives join as so many more mobile parts, so many human extensions of nonhuman processes conforming their personal traits and tempos to the anonymous drive and impersonal sequences of the anonymous machine. By contrast, the agricultural laborer is like the craftsman, a whole person, all of whose day life includes the consummatory consciousness which industry relegates to the freedoms of the night. Again, the product of the operative is likewise anonymous, its raw material reaching him he need not and does not care whence or from whom, the finished product leaving with no mark of his own personality upon it, to be sold by somebody he does not know to somebody else he has no interest in, for money a percentage of which he will find in his wage envelope.

The money touches him more nearly; it brings him feelings of reassurance, of liberation, even of power. But its prime meaning is not those feelings. Its prime meaning is the productions and services of other men that he can exchange that money for. His manhood discloses itself in the exchange; his neighbor's dignity and worth as man, as well as his own, must look back to the work of the day as foundation for the leisure of the night. Work is cause, leisure is only consequence. The vocations of the world are the life of the world, and its cultures utter them as a peacock's tail utters the bird's vitality. Labor is neither slavery nor penance, it is knowledge, skill and value, the content of delight. As Ruskin wrote: "When men are rightly occupied, their amusement grows out of their work, as the colour of petals out of a fruitful flower." The dignity of labor, thence is of a nobler, more living kind than the dignities of leisure. A culture pertains to, and expresses this dignity which shall liberate labor from the indignities imposed upon it by the culture of the leisure class, and shall at last bring it to that refinement and expression of its inward being which is destined to vindicate the dignity of labor in its wholeness and integrity. This liberating culture is Proletcult.

X

The word is, I think, an invention of Eden and Cedar Paul, and entitles a book they published in the early twenties of the present century. They projected Proletcult as "a fighting culture aiming at the overthrow of capitalism, and at the replacement of democratic culture and bourgeois ideology by ergocratic culture and proletarian ideology." Like other young people of that decade, they were excited by what they had read and heard about the Bolshevik revolution in Russia, like the Sidney Webbs taking its pretensions for performance, and its words for events. That their "ergocratic culture and proletarian ideology" was but another "opiate of the people" competing with elder brothers for dominion; that both phrases were but symbols and slogans of the Lenino-Stalinite march through blood and death to power, the Proletcultist's enamored faith could neither note nor concede. Nor could they recognize that the personality-images, which channeled workingmen's ambitions and desires, were still the forms of force, freedom, and fulfillment that tradition communicated and the neighborhood supplied.

These also the hierarchies of Kremlin commissars took over, willy-nilly, from their "bourgeois" opposite numbers. Dress, diet, comforts, protocols, housing, transportation, entertainment—in everything but manners—they emulated the ruling hierarchies of the condemned "bourgeois" world. The latter are the Joneses of the Soviet élite. But in manners they have maintained a vituperative rudeness which is the signature of their Proletcult. It contrasts sharply, not only with the amenities of intercourse of the "bourgeois," but also with the traditional courtesy of the Russian peoples, and of all simple peoples whose working and living are so interdependent.

In the culture of the West, a change of the people's status as "labor" had been in process for nearly two centuries. During the years between the transvaluations of labor already performed by Rousseau, by Ruskin, by Proudhon and Fourier, by Robert Owen, by Karl Marx, by the various Marxian factions, and the theory and practice of Proletcult, the words "worker," "workingman" had become loaded with transvaluing connotations which rendered them rivals of the denotations of the words "gentleman," "lady." They are often pronounced with the praiseful unction customarily given such words as "Christian," "the Virgin," "God." This usage becomes de rigueur in Proletcult. It signalizes no abolition of traditional distinctions such as Hellene and barbarian, Jew and Gentile, Christian and infidel exemplify. It signalizes only transposing place-holders in the hierarchies of power and privilege. It signalizes little change in the numbers of the monopolists who possess "the fullness and beauty of life" in abundance, nor of the deprived to whom it is no less scarce than to their ancestors. As in the social life of the barnyard, the chickens come and go but the order of pecking goes on regardless, so the doctrine that culture and vocation are antipathetic remains as orthodox in the lands of proletcultists as in any "bourgeois" culture.

But, in order to vindicate the ruthless and bloody translocations of power to defend its privileged beneficiaries from their own overthrow, a sadistic policing of all forms of association was installed, and was rationalized by forbidding or eradicating the symbols and images of the traditional culture, rigidly censoring opinion, the arts, and the sciences into conformity with the creed and code of Proletcult. In *1984*, George Orwell stripped naked its logic and logistic; the foregone conclusion that every totalitarian ruler, secular Big Brother or sacerdotal Holy Father, must overtly or covertly assume infallibility in order to rationalize its irrational authority, Orwell's image is Big Brother's "Ministry of Truth." Its task is constantly to alter the records of the past so that they suit the changing practices of the power-holders as they act in such wise as to stay in power. Their directive is the apothegm: *Who controls the past controls the future; who controls the present controls the past.* Their medium is *Newspeak,* a language whose old words receive new meanings confirming and sanctioning the rule of Big Brother and his hierarchies as eternal and universal and unique.

Proletcult, it will be seen, whether as aspiration or as achievement, perpetuates the invidious distinction between culture and vocation intrinsic to the tradition but dresses it up in different images and symbols, and encodes it in different parables.

XI

Nevertheless, the nineteenth and twentieth centuries not only witnessed challenges to the distinction, but took account of studies whose findings would, other things being equal, have wiped it out. While literary critics, educators and revolutionists were propounding, defending, reordering yet perpetuating the distinction, skeptical and curious men went far

from home, not as missioners for ways of life and thought of
their own societies, but to see, to understand, and to account
for the different ethos of diverse simpler peoples in Africa, in
Australia, in North and South America, in the islands of the
Pacific. These students of the ways and works of men came
to be called anthropologists. An upshot of their inquiries was
the notion that the vocations of a community were the nu-
cleus of its culture; that their relations were reciprocal and
compenetrative; that if consumption was end and production
means, it was the means nevertheless which gave substance and
form to the end; that the mores which segregated them from
one another are mores of predation menacing to both the
culture and its supporting vocations. The initiation of this
alternative denotation of culture was Edward Tylor's. His
pioneering work, *Primitive Culture*, includes in culture, which
he holds interchangeable with civilization, the "knowledge,
beliefs, arts, morals, customs, and any other capabilities and
habits acquired by man as a member of society."

That is, a group's culture embraces the total economy of
their life together. It includes in a configuration striving ever
to preserve an ongoing stability, all diversities of scenes and
stuffs, of raw materials and the knowledge and workmanship
that process them, all the generations of men and women and
children as they grow up in concords and discords, all their
collective and personal remembrances, embodied in rites and
rotes, myths, legends and prophecies. The group may be a
family, a clan, a tribe, a nationality, a church, an industry, a
state, a nation, a guild, a scientific society, a baseball club, or
any other organization for sport or play; or any association
of these. If it lasts long enough to generate a tradition, it will
have shaped itself into a collectivity with a cultural individuality peculiar to itself. Once established, individuals may enter
such a group by birth, by immigration, by initiation, by compulsion, or any mode you will of preparation for and commitment to the identifying participation. The various modes of
entry and commitment are signalized as conversion, indoctrination, education, acculturation, naturalization. Individuals
may leave the group by death, by liberation, by emigration,
by expulsion, or any mode of separation or of alienation you
will. However they come and go, appear or disappear, others

composing the group will be there before them and continue after them. The group culture will seem to have a nature independent of them all; to be a whole different from its parts, with ways and works evincing its own different laws of persistence, struggle and growth, and capable of determination without reference to the dynamic specificity of the parts. If the individuals of the culture are psychosomatic organisms, the culture is a superorganic psychosoma which conforms and acculturates to itself all who enter it, however they enter it. It is their overruling providence, the shaper of their fates and fortunes, with a cyclical life history peculiar to itself. The new word for the study and exposition of cultural totalities so conceived is culturology.

The relations of these cultures to one another, their concords and discords, are thence also independent variables, not necessarily affected by the residual network of relationships, political and other, with which they are interwoven. Florian Znaniecki, renewing Mazzini for today, observes that "a solidary human collectivity of hundreds, of thousands, even millions of people who share the same culture can exist for a long time without a common political government" . . . That "national cultural societies" are found in many lands, he argues, indicates that politics is not enough, that cultures are essential, that world peace can come only as the world's people unite into a "world culture society" creating a "world culture."[1] F. C. S. Northrop underscores the observation that "it is culturalism rather than nationalism that is the rising fact of the world today," and that the road to peace is the road of cultural parity developing in "an intercultural co-operation that should provide a sure passage from western colonialism and Asiatic revolt."[2]

[1] Florian W. Znaniecki: *Modern Nationalities: a Sociological Study*. 1952. University of Illinois Press.
[2] F. C. S. Northrop: *The Taming of the Nations. A Study of the Cultural Bases of International Policy*. New York 1952.

CONCERNING VARIETIES
OF PLURALISM *

"Cultural Pluralism" is a controversial expression. It has been such from the day it first figured in the public prints. Now, after two generations, the view of human nature, human relations and the human enterprise which it signalizes is still either rationalistically disputed or passionately rejected. Disputation and rejection are scientific or creedal or both together. The creedal modes project some species of totalitarianism—racial, sacerdotal, communist, fascist or other. The scientific modes postulate some sort of monistic sociological theory employing concepts of organism and other models frequent among social scientists. Scientific may transpose to creedal, and vice versa, whenever a working hypothesis, subject to revision according to the testimony of events and the alterations of time, is transvalued into a doctrinal system always and everywhere the same; or when such a system is released into a working hypothesis altering as it works. The attitude of the believer, not the monism he believes in, decides; and the attitude may often take shape as an unequal commingling of both.

Of course, that the expression, "cultural pluralism" brings out antagonisms, would be prima-facie evidence that there *are* alternatives in culture and that these involve more than a distinction without a difference; that they are reliably plural. Surely, if the cultures of mankind were one and only one, alternatives of it could not be, or even be thought. But monists of every species are regularly engaged in waging a total war against alternatives. On the intellectual front they are perennially proving that what is not *their* culture either is no culture, or is unreal, unworthy, and impotent. On the social front, they mobilize force to keep their peoples incommunicado to

* A version of this chapter was published in *The New Negro Thirty Years After*. Howard University Press, 1955, Washington, D.C.

alternatives in every institution of the common life. Each
totalitarianism represents itself as the Absolute One, in which
all power, goodness, rightness, truth and beauty are indivisibly
at one. With its rivals, each is a group in a collection of collec-
tives whose relations are reciprocally inimical and destructive.
Their togetherness adds up to a war of all against all.

Could any of these ones succeed in abolishing all its rivals,
it would thereupon become in fact the absolute one-with-no-
other that it pretends to be in imagination. As Spinoza had
argued long ago, a universal nature all one must be a universal nature all alone, self-contained and self-containing, with
no future, no past, no history, no neighbors, no relations. Any
entity having a history, neighbors, relations, a past and a future
can at best possess only secondary, derivative being with
neither existence nor value in and for itself. At worst, it must
be sheer illusion and nothingness. Reality must needs be one
eternal universal substance, manifest behind and through the
infinite multitude of diversities that appear and pass and lapse
back into the ultimate power, bliss and knowledge which are
one as the eternal Oneness.

It is an old story that reasoning of this sort only translates
the actual pluralism of our experience into one or another of
the many symbolic monisms of our discourse, and that our
discourse bespeaks conditions we hunger for and aspire to, far
more than conditions we acknowledge and endure. And on the
record, no culture hungers for the same goods and forms or
embodies its aspirations in the same expressions; the One of
each one's desire is a different One. On the record, the *terminus ad quem* of the cultures of mankind turns out to be no
less a pluralism than their *terminus a quo*. Thus, the "One
World" of political and economic agitation can be one only as
a union on equal terms of sovereign and independent diversities
alone whose agreement could make and keep it thus one; who
make themselves thus one, and stay so, only so long as they
agree on the oneness. Thus, the One universe of our sciences
and philosophies and religions is also but a Uni-verse; literally
a *turning to* oneness, not a oneness already existing and perceived. The oneness they turn to must similarly start from
plurality and can live only as the associative pattern which
this plurality consent to. Unity here names a future formation

we desirefully steer our present imaginations toward; the togetherness we now acquiescingly experience is a changing
aggregation, not unity unalterable.

Western culture spans an ongoing conflict between aspiration and acquiescence, which might be appraised as the West's
struggle for unity. Wars over differing cultures are events of
this struggle, and no less such are the pretensions of the cults
and the speculations of the philosophies, each with its own
dream of unanimity or empire.

Interludes occur, however, when kings and priests and their
poets and theologians become disillusioned about projects of
universal dominion and totalitarian culture; when prophets
and sages become disillusioned about an absolute One, to be
disclosed behind the veil of multitude and diversity. Interludes
occur when thinkers not only acquiesce in the latter, but prize
them and yearn to keep their singularities forever real; real,
however, as so many absolutes existing eternally in perfect
harmony with one another, each free within from all relations,
tensions and conflicts and desiring to be nothing but what it
is, and to possess nothing but what it possesses. Heaven is, by
definition, such a perfect society; in the Father's house are
many mansions, but they are the mansions of one and only
one culture. That there are other heavens with other cultures,
each a unity specific to the need of another cult, would not
affect the monistic passion of the true believer. He would
wage war against those other Heavens and denounce them as
Hells. But if he is also a philosopher, he might appraise the
heavenly mansions as each an irreducible unit, self-containing
and self-contained. He would then be a pluralist; but his
pluralism would be a pluralism of absolutes. His absolutes might
be material particles, each a one beyond all division and
anatomy, inwardly impervious to every impact and external
to every relation. Or his absolutes might be spiritual entities,
immortal souls, whose knowing is only remembering, whom
learning cannot alter, nor experience teach. Plato imagined the
inner self as such an Absolute, and the Christian doctors followed Plato.

But the notable modern pluralism of this sort is the one
invented by the seventeenth-century philosophical genius,
Gottfried Wilhelm Leibnitz. It also originated in experienced

difficulties and culminated in a transcendental system which demotes the empirical realities that bred it into sterile unrealities powerless even to be. Leibnitz was a German and a Protestant of great intellectual ingenuity and imaginative perception. His scientific achievements were paralleled by his political endeavors. He disputed with Newton the invention of the calculus. He designed and demonstrated a logic machine. He was an apostle of the new science and agitated for the organization of royal scientific societies by the monarchies of Europe. From Jesuit missionaries, he learned about the Chinese and about the reciprocal tolerance and conciliation among their diverse religions characteristic of their culture. He had the idea that China might have been the cradle of civilization, and the Chinese language its mother tongue. He thought the stuff of a universal language might be found in Chinese and he labored to devise one on his own. Chinese ways in religion seemed to him a possible model for Christian to change to, since the latter were so much ways of war between church and church. He projected a unification of Protestant and Catholic.

Of course, his project got nowhere. In Christian Europe plurality stayed *un*-unifiable. And if there, in all likelihood, everywhere. Ultimately both the calculus of measure and the analysis of matter end up at singularities, each indivisible, simple, having no extension and no duration, yet each a unique this-and-no-other, impenetrable to all otherness. Consider the study of space. Does not space turn out to be a continuum of dimensionless points of position, every one different and every one exclusive of every other? Do not those reciprocally impenetrable entities without dimension compound into the three dimensions we discern as the extended being, Space? Time and thoughts and things likewise atomize into patterns and sequences of unique, simple entities. What are they, then? Our nearest, surest experience of them is experience of ourselves. Indeed, in the nature of things, it is, it must be, our sole experience. And its vital center is the effort and tension we are conscious of as our awareness enlarges, from the dark passivity and inertia of unawareness when asleep or "swooning," to the luminously aware propulsion and clearness and distinctness of utter wakefulness. The span of consciousness, whatever its degree, is a self-containing and self-contained energy—matter when asleep, spirit when awake—existing incommunicado, in itself and for itself, influencing none, uninfluenced by any, of its infinity of fellows; it is a force without doors or windows. Leibnitz' name for it is Monad. Since, nevertheless, we Monads are conscious of an environment, ideas of environment must be innate and rightly representative, because God ordained a pre-established harmony between ourselves and our fellows of whom otherwise we can have no awareness of any kind. Monads are to one another like so many different clocks set by their maker to keep the same time forever.

Here we have an absolutistic pluralism. Leibnitz' philosophy of nature, man and human destiny postulates pluralism, thus, as a way of both rationalizing and compensating somehow the failures of his own endeavors to compromise and conciliate warring states and churches. In the history of cultures such pluralism seems to be invoked when an imperial drive of whatever kind is contained, when opposed forces are so equal that they bound without apparently changing one another. The terms of foreign policy for such reciprocal isolation are sometimes "cold war," sometimes "co-existence," sometimes even "co-prosperity." In domestic affairs the terms are sometimes "separate but equal," sometimes simply "pluralism." An instance of this isolationist pluralism is the pluralism of state and church sometimes argued by the Roman Catholic establishment for the United States, although with considerable modifications to the advantage of the Romanist interest.

That the pluralism is ever a design, never an achievement, we have already noted. The perceived Monad—individual, collective or hierarchal—does have doors and windows. It does learn and change, as it experiences and lives. Its knowledge is not merely recollection; it is discovery and recollection only of discovery. It does sustain its identity by communication, not by segregation. Leibnitz could find no *tertium quid* to the alternative between Monism such as Spinoza's and his own Monadism, because he was unwilling to take experience for what it was. His Monadism was never even a near rival of the dominant Monism whose varieties so largely impattern the diverse enterprises composing a civilization. And Monisms cultivated by most social institutions have consistently figured as aggressive intentions far more than assured achievements. Overtly and covertly, the spontaneous pluralism of nature and history keep dispelling every imposed unity by diversification and withdrawal within, by breaching and penetration without. What preponderant force openly suppresses, the liberty-craving spirit hiddenly expresses. What it is forbidden openly to disclose and avow, it secretly smuggles and bootlegs. What it cannot counter in strength, it counters in symbol. Its agents are allegory and laughter. It accomplishes the ends of communicating the not-to-be-communicated by such means as the Revelation of St. John in the New Testament, or the tales and essays of Rabelais, or M. de Voltaire, or Daniel Defoe or Jonathan Swift or Anatole France, or Aldous Huxley or Mark Twain or George Orwell. If a single, simple meaning is not safe, a *double entendre* is insurance, and sometimes profit as well.

Only since the Democratic Revolution has a philosophical pluralism come to the mature expression which acquiesces in this spontaneous pluralism and shapes it into working hypotheses concerning the relations between the Many and the One in nature and in the affairs of mankind, that is, in the cultures which are the all of the human enterprise. This pluralism also postulates individuality, particularity, as primal; it also could be said to understand man and nature in monadic terms. But it neither deprives the human person of his dynamic relations with his neighbors, nor converts the ever-ongoing communications between them to a preordained ineluctable harmony. On the contrary, it recognizes that the relations do really relate without identifying; that the communications do truly inform and persuade without coercing. It signalizes them as the ways that people who are different from one another do, in fact, come together and move apart, forming and dissolving the groups and societies wherewith they secure to one another their diverse safety and happiness. This pluralism is the kind intrinsic to the Cultural Pluralism always and everywhere characterizing men's undertakings. It is what the Democratic Idea intends, and what the philosophy of Cultural Pluralism designates as the cultural ideal natural to a free world. This pluralism also purposes One World, but One World *in pluribus*, as a federal union of diversities, not a diversion of diversities into undifferentiated unity.

Let us at once concede that this kind of pluralism does not make any easier the task of the culturologist or any other technician of the sciences of society. Sciences postulate the oneness of the many in two modes. One is exemplified by a repetition of identicals such that, at long last, repetition is condensed in a continuing sameness, wherewith past and future, presence and prophecy are One Given in every scientific "law." The other is exemplified by a whole or totality whose parts are so related to one another that none can exist or alter independently of the others, and none have any force or meaning save in consequence of the organic whole which grows and sheds it as a beast grows and sheds its hairs, or a fowl its feathers. Such wholes are sometimes called *In-groups* and their neighbors, friendly or unfriendly, are distinguished from them as *Out-groups. In* and *Out* denote how the individual parts constituting the wholes relate to one another. The words signalize interaction, present or lacking. When present, the interaction so connects the parts with one another that each acquires a sense of linkage to all, a feeling of belonging and interdependence, with respect to which individuals not so linked are perceived as outsiders, foreign, strange, and dangerous. Words such as *team, club, factory, family, church, union* are words of belongingness and linkage. They denote boundaries between *ins* and *outs.* Other symbols and images may signalize these boundaries, which the bounded create for themselves by their relations to one another. Such boundaries may be called autogenous. Creeds and codes may delineate them. Natural or artificial demarcations of landscape, guarded as borders between any two regions of group habitation, may define them. However diverse in themselves be the boundaries, they resemble each other in that they shape up the group's life-space and delineate the formations and fields of its culture.

As such, boundaries are, of course, artifacts. They are not like an animal's skin. They exist only in virtue of the ends and instrumentalities of the individual forces who maintain, respect and defend them against penetration by outsiders. Actually, individuals keep disregarding boundaries, whether geographical or cultural. They keep passing out of some group they are in into some other group they are out of. Actually, the more "culture" any of them has acquired, the more liberal or general his education has been, the fuller is his awareness of the values of the *Out-groups*, the freer are his powers to avail himself of them, and the more abundant are his means wherewith to comprehend and enjoy them. His equipment constitutes his cultural mobility; it renders him, mind and body, a cosmopolitan, literally a citizen of the world. Without ever losing his commitment to his home base, his citizenship, and his original culture, he is now also no stranger in any different country and culture.[1]

Moreover, his mobility between different cultures is an extension of his mobility within his cultural home base. He can move without strain, and with satisfaction, from one to another of the many and multiplying organizations of interests whereof the culture of his country consists, without having to become "acculturated" to the different and "deculturated" from the same of his primal commitment and allegiance.

Indeed, as victims of catastrophe, social or natural, well know, this mobility within a culture and between culture and culture, can be taken for a measure of the tempo and rate of cultural change; and whether a person survives his culture, or his culture survives the person. Sciences of culture prefer, as perhaps they must, to postulate the latter. Without self-repeating identicals, without constants, how could they be sciences at all? Hence cultures may be many, but scientific method is held to require that each should be thought as a constant, at least a continuum, whose repetitions may be measured and foretold, and whose nonrepeating variations may be either liquidated in the repetitions or disregarded as irrelevancies. Cultures so thought are stable configurations of human living whose patterns precede and survive the individuals entering them by birth, immigration, or however, and leaving them by death, emigration, expulsion, catastrophe or however. Cultures so thought are enduring orders of behavior whereto individuals are tangent episodes.

[1] Cf. Gandhi: "I want the winds of all cultures to blow freely about my house, but not to be swept off my feet by any."

No matter, then, how long the time, how prolonged the history, every culture has a singularity of faith and form that is one and the same from its archaeological beginnings to its actual or still future end. Call this identity, common creed, nationality, national spirit, or anything which denotes a fundamental invariancy and continuity. Concurrent with it and within it, there are also the variations, the nonrecurrent identities which don't repeat, which cannot be arrested, coalesced and prophesied about. These are the people, the individuals who make and break the cultures they pass into and out of. They are the true subject matter of history when history is historical. Each is a span of time from birth to death, wherein his determined past works in his present to determine his undetermined future. His future is truly future in so far as it does not repeat his past and cannot be foretold from his past. His growing up and growing old is a line of animal change to which the cultural variations and innovations, not the animal and cultural repetitions, give human significance. It is those which compound into his personal history and aggregate the stuff of his biography. They signalize his uniqueness as a person, even as a group's history signalizes its group-personality by the variations and innovations that compenetrate to form its culture. Both personal biography and group history are formations presenting the impact on one another of recurrent and unique events.

Now this interplay of recurrences and uniquenesses is the experiential source of the philosopher's persistent "problem" of the One and the Many, Pluralism and Monism, Collectivism and Individualism, Organicity and Association, and so on, in pairs too boring to count. Which of any pair can be most fruitfully used to explain, say, British personality, British culture through British literature? Conceive a chronological series starting with Chaucer. Trace a literary trajectory from Chaucer to Shakespeare, from Shakespeare to Milton, from Milton to Pope, from Pope to Tennyson, from Tennyson to T. S. Eliot. These poets can hardly be said to be repetitions of one another. A critical study of them designed to elicit a composite image which accents recurrence and blurs variation could be nothing more than another variant with unintended and unanticipated features, that might serve as an instrument for thinking these incommensurables into a self-contained unity. But it could neither identify their diversity nor neutralize its own character as diversification. Actually, the critic starts with the diversities of time, place, occasion, temperament and context as data. He takes them as he finds them and does not look behind them. He undertakes his criticism as a labor of identification. It is identification, not differentiation, which we all have mostly to work at, seeking that easement of life and living which a common principle, rule or law has been known to bring, and which is so regularly equated to insight and understanding.

Unhappily, in our experience, whatever stays truly always and everywhere the same stays null and dead. What exists and lives, struggles to go on doing so, and its struggle is its change. A living culture is a changing culture; and it is a changing culture, and not an auctioneer's storage house or an archaeologist's dump of fragments, fossils and ruins, because of the transactions wherewith living, altering, individuals transform old thoughts and things while laboring to preserve them and to produce new. Cultures live and grow in and through the individual, and their vitality is a function of individual diversities of interests and associations. Pluralism is the *sine qua non* of their persistence and prosperous growth. But not the absolutist pluralism which the concept of the unaltering and inalterable Monad discloses. On the contrary, the *sine qua non* is fluid, relational pluralism which the living individual encounters in the transactions wherewith he constructs his personal history moving out of groups and into groups, engaging in open or hidden communion with societies of his fellows, every one different from the others, and all teamed together, and struggling to provide and maintain the common means which nourish, assure, enhance, the different, and often competing, values they differently cherish.

CULTURE AND THE AMERICAN IDEA

I. MONISTIC ONENESS

By and large, the Ones which our hearts crave and our minds assert turn out on closer inspection to be either unifications which we effect, or self-disclosing free unions produced by the many as they affect each other. Whether we probe to the invisible stars of the heavens with ever mightier telescopes, or to the indiscernible atoms of the earth with ever more discriminating microscopes, or with ever more powerful rupturing cyclotrons, the One we first perceive or postulate gives way and is replaced by an unperceived and unwanted Many. Probing cultures and civilizations comes to a like end. The unities turn out to be contractions of distance, like the skylines of cities that seem simple, smooth, without a break when remote, and show up complex, rough, turbulent, precipitous and tangled on near approach. Histories are likewise contractions of distance, the near times vertiginous, violent, evil, the far times generally utopian "good old days." The current age feels deeply that its own is the "Age of Anxiety." A hundred years from now, an epigon of the guild of history-writers writing of mid-century United States, will in all probability see the instant excitements of these days over communists and atom bombs, espionage and mccarthyism, cold war and Third World War as a skyline in whose smooth pattern the crags and peaks are flattened and the abysses bridged; the immediately experienced anger, terror, and disgust smoothed to a calm perspective by vision and correct taste, their poignancies transvalued into trivialities in virtue of their distance from the interpreter's *now*. He might even appraise those poignancies as no quality of events or persons perceived; as only a lack of courage in us perceiving, so that we ourselves paralyze our power to see them as they are and deal with them as they deserve. Lack of courage may be a cultural attitude with which leaders infect followers and elders children. When an age is signalized as an age of anxiety it is thereby signalized as an age without courage.

For ages of culture are often tagged with the moods and attitudes which the poets and sages and prophets we take for their voices predominantly convey. They are typed: ages of faith, dark ages, romantic age, age of the enlightenment, machine age, as if they were this and only this. The typings, by historians or philosophers or men of art alike, purport to utter a unity discovered, while at most they bespeak a unification desired and more or less encompassed, among the power-holders of the age. Or else they signify a writer's transvaluation of the age's confusing diversities into an ordered identity less taxing to his mind and art. In and of itself, no man's, no society's experience exemplifies any one order. Individuals and groups struggle to render some chosen order dominant, straining and striving to convert the unique into the repetitive and the lapsing into the continuing. They would bend into cyclical orbits the straight lines and parabolas of ongoing change. They would transfigure the dead into the resurrected or the immortal. Multitude exacts from us fearful vigilance and imposes endless tasks wherefrom Aloneness frees us. This may be why there is that in each of us which impels toward authoritarian totalitarianisms; why the ideal One God of the theologians is God Alone, God without a like. One's experience often harvests from isolation a peace and security no association yields. If then, the doors and windows of selfhood willy-nilly keep it open to the outside it must win isolation either by forcefully shutting out and cutting off the Outsider, or by consuming every form of Otherness in the Self's own identity, putting an end to difference altogether. It should be already clear enough that this never gets done. But knowing that it never gets done has been no hindrance to trying to do it; hope springs eternal that *this* time at last disaster will not consummate failure, if failure willy-nilly comes. Hence, Mankind's catholicisms, political and sacerdotal, and the perennial wars of the faiths.

II. IMAGES AND SYMBOLS OF THE AMERICAN IDEA

Now unifications occur which are neither authoritarian nor totalitarian, which neither excommunicate nor consume, but invite, preserve and encourage diversity. Entirely in aspiration, not a little in performance, the American Idea envisions and intends one such unification. The struggle to transact it from an article of faith into the eventuations of history is the vital center of American Culture.

The American Idea ushers in a cultural ideal. Like all ideals it is at once a philosophy of existence, a program of human relations and a code of action. Each and all, in their singularities and configurations, are uttered by images, by symbols and by reasoned statements which disclose, not "the American dream" but the American faith that the works of Americanism are loyal undertakings to embody the faith in fact. Like all ideals for which mankind work and fight, the American Idea is a present wager on the formation of a future which may well not come off. It is no bet on a sure thing, but a hazard with no hedge, of lives, fortunes and sacred honor. In those for whom the bet is religion, it strengthens the will, alerts the understanding and exalts the heart; it invests their struggle to live with a brightness no misadventure succeeds in diminishing; it enables them to confront death and suffering with courage, and the most frightening foe with firmness that never yields; it penetrates the dullest routine with translumining perspectives and a quiet joy. The lives of such believers become signalized by the quality of progress, that process of habituation and innovation wherein the going creates its own direction and the goal is itself the movement without bounds.

Of the uttering images—all the compenetration of diverse figures, living out actual or imaginary lives in places as diverse as a New England village, a Midwest prairie, a Northern lake region, a Southern swamp or desert, or a Far Western forest— the most widely known today is Uncle Sam. Uncle Sam is a peer of Britain's John Bull and of other such concretions of an ethos or a culture, today's avatars of the ancient gods, with perhaps qualities of human leadership deified in their fleshless being: qualities of Confucius or Caesar or Jesus or Washington or Lincoln. Alternative images are patron saints or national gods. Many other *dramatis personae* have been consumed in the making of Uncle Sam than national leaders. There is Yankee Doodle in him and Dan'l Boone and Johnny Appleseed and Paul Bunyan and Tom Sawyer and Huck Finn, to say nothing of the Yankee at King Arthur's Court.

Sometimes the image is the figure of a bird or beast like the Gallic rooster or the Russian bear or the British lion: the character given the animal is read as the character of the culture. Less perceptive projections are heraldic devices and symbols on seals and coins. Very generally flags[1] are such. But all are intended to be somehow instant communications of some preferred aspect of a common ethos, its principles or its practices. Where efficacious, they stand as the visible presence of the unseen diversities of an entire tradition, evoking and renewing their user's faith, reawakening his awareness of historic commitment to union and co-operation.

The sense of history, the present feeling of things past, is here focal. For whatever determination we can give the undetermined future must, for its matters and methods, turn upon the past and alter it. What else is education, or art, or any other formation of the human enterprise but such a way not only of using, but using up the past?

III. THE AMERICAN IDEA—TWO INSIGHTS

Now let us first consider the image of America in the perception of two Americans of diverse origins and fortunes, who, three generations apart, told what they learned "America" meant to feeling and hope. The first is the novelist, Henry James. In 1867 he was living in Europe, full of his plans for his career as a man of letters, and the more aware of the Amer-

---

[1] We might recall Daniel Webster's denotation of the American flag as conveyor of the American Idea in the peroration of his famous Reply to Hayne: "When my eyes shall be turned to behold for the last time the sun in heaven, may I not see him shining on the broken and dishonored fragments of a once glorious Union, on States dissevered, discordant, belligerent! On a land rent with civil feud, or drenched, it may be, in fraternal blood! Let their last feeble and lingering glance rather behold the gorgeous ensign of the Republic, now known and honored throughout the earth, still high advanced, its arms and trophies streaming in their original lustre; not a stripe erased or polluted, not a single star obscured; bearing for its motto no such miserable interrogatory as 'What is all this worth?' Nor these other words of delusion and folly, 'Liberty first and union afterwards'; but everywhere, spread all over in characters of living light, blazing on its ample folds, as they float over the sea and over the land, and in every wind under the whole heavens, that other sentiment, dearer to every American heart, 'Liberty and Union, now and forever, one and inseparable.'"

ica of his day because he was living in Europe. He wrote to his
intimate friend, T. S. Perry:

By this constant exchange and comparison of feelings and
ideas, by the wear and tear of living and talking and observing,
works of art shape themselves into completeness. One feels we
young Americans are, without cant, men of the future. I feel that
my only chance for success as a critic is to let all the breezes of
the West blow through me at their will. We are Americans born
—il faut prendre son parti. I look upon it as a great blessing, and I
think that to be an American, is an excellent preparation for culture. We have exquisite qualities as a race, and it seems to me that
we are ahead of the European races in the fact that more than
either of them we can deal freely with forms of civilization not
our own, can choose and assimilate, and in short, aesthetically, etc.,
claim our property where we find it. To have no national stamp
has hitherto been a regret and a drawback, but I think it not un-
likely that American writers may yet indicate that a vast intellectual fusion and synthesis of various national tendencies of the
world is the condition of more important achievements than any
we have seen. We must, of course, have something of our own—
something distinctive and homogeneous, and I take it that one
shall find it in our moral consciousness, our unprecedented spiritual lightness and vigor. In this sense at least we shall have a
national cachet. I expect nothing great during your lifetime or
mine, perhaps; but my instincts quite agree with yours in looking
to see something original and beautiful disengage itself from our
ceaseless fermentation and turmoil. You see, I am willing to leave
it a matter of instinct. God speed the day.

Almost half a century later, Henry James, American all his
life, committed to the American Idea, felt that this spiritual
allegiance required him to change his political allegiance from
the United States to the United Kingdom. The Idea laid down
the perspectives within which this artist of the written word
could perfect his art. Its center is the moral consciousness of a
people who had fought over human slavery as principle and
practice in a bloody and costly war; into this center it could
draw, and "deal freely with" the entirety of the diverse cultures of the world, sure that at last "something original and
beautiful will disengage itself."

From the aspirations of emigrant Henry James in 1867 let
us turn now to the sentiments of immigrant Italians almost nine

decades later. They are written down in a report which Nicholas Tucci first published in the *New Yorker* of August, 1951—under the general title, *The Underground Letters*— of talks and imaginings of Italian immigrants whose more youthful relatives were bringing them to the United States. Mr. Tucci writes:

. . . And the word that turned up most frequently in their conversation was, "America." In colloquial Italian, "America" had come to mean something more than a geographical place. It is by extension, any deposit of hopes, any tabernacle where all things too big, too difficult, too far beyond one's grasp take shape, become true— so true that all one needs in order to touch them is a ship that will take one there. "America" is, again, something one finds or makes, a stepping-stone, a rung in the ladder that allows one to climb a little higher—not, of course, in the country called America, but back home. "America" also means the treasure one finds when "America" (the rung in the ladder) is steadily under one's feet. Inevitably, the question that the old people ask one another over and over is, "Is America *America?*"

That is, Is America an incarnation of the American Idea?

The question opposes America the geographical, political, economic formation, with its people's institutions and behaviors, to America, the substance of things hoped for, the evidence of things not seen, America the Fact and America the Idea. It focuses, even as Henry James's forecast focuses, on the Idea of America. The phrase is Theodore Parker's. A minister of religion and an Abolitionist, this New Englander addressed an Anti-slavery convention at a meeting held in Boston on May 29, 1850. In the course of it he said:

There is what I call the American Idea. This idea demands as the proximate organization thereof, a democracy—that is, a government of all the people, by all the people, for all the people: of course a government on the principles of eternal justice, the unchanging law of God: for shortness' sake I will call it the idea of Freedom.

IV. THE DECLARATION OF INDEPENDENCE

In the back of the speaker's mind, as of the minds of all that time's communicants of the religion of America, such as Ralph Waldo Emerson, or Henry Thoreau or Herman Melville, or

Walt Whitman, or Abraham Lincoln, was the declaration of faith with which the American Idea was spoken forth before mankind, and which since the turn of the century has been in America far less invoked and far less bespoken. I refer of course to the Declaration of Independence. The American credo consists of the "truths" by which it warrants the separation of the colonies from the United Kingdom. They are its articles of faith, and their configuration is the American Idea. What else could they intend but the freedom which Theodore Parker affirmed, which Henry James postulated, which Nicholas Tucci connoted?

Now it is well to have in mind that the writers and signers of the Declaration, the minority of natives and the handful of volunteer strangers who fought the American War of Independence to victory, held these truths to be "self-evident," and that these self-evident truths made the human condition then everywhere prevailing a contradiction and overruling of that self-evidence. If the conditions were a fact, the truths were a Big Lie. If the truths were valid, the condition must needs be a hateful perversion of truth and a rebellion against God's will.

For to a world of peoples everywhere dominated by considerations of privilege based on differences of birth, rank, wealth, race, creed, and occupation, the Declaration said, all men are created equal. To societies whose folkways and mores required not only submission of the weak to the strong, but varied alienations from the weak of "life, liberty and the pursuit of happiness," the Declaration said those are equally every man's unalienable rights, inherent, constitutive of his humanity. To a world where government, every kind of government, government of a household, a clan, a village, a city, a church, a school, a state, an empire justified its powers and authority by claiming to have received them directly from God, and therefore always to be submitted to, obeyed and reverenced, without question or dissent, the Declaration said that government is a means and not an end, a servant, not a master; that its duties are to "secure these rights"; that it receives its powers and authority directly from the governed; that it governs by their consent; that when government neglects or fails to perform the services for which it was devised, becoming "destructive of these ends" they who instituted it may "alter or abolish it" and replace it with "new government," that in their belief will perform more aptly and loyally the task for which it was devised.

In the congeries of societies to whom the Declaration was addressed, tradition, law, and custom invested certain selected groups with liberties and powers, rights and privileges denied to others because of their parentage; because they were women; because they were Protestant or Catholic or Jew or Moslem or deist or agnostic or atheist; because they were farmers or manual laborers, because they were poor, and for a diversity of other causes. They were penalized for what they were, the great majority thus different from the chosen minorities. To all the Declaration affirmed the parity of the different and the unalienability of the equal rights of the different freely to live, and to struggle for the life and the happiness which its singularity envisions and projects. Is it remarkable that to minds which prized the "facts of life" above the aspirations of the livers, this affirmation could be at best what Rufus Choate had called it, a collection of "glittering generalities," or what George Santayana called it, "a piece of literature, a salad of illusions"? That, at worst, it must needs be a subversion of the law and order of all society and thus a rebellion against the God whose providence nature discloses and the state of things-as-they-are exemplifies? [1]

---

[1] Times of anxiety can repristinate this judgment also among Americans to whom the Declaration has been taught as the Word made flesh in the American nation. Thus, on July 4, 1951, the *Capital Times* of Madison, Wisconsin, sent reporters to secure signatures "to a petition consisting exclusively of sections from the Declaration of Independence and the Bill of Rights." Only one of one hundred and twelve spoken to signed. The rest were afraid. Some denounced the petition as "communist stuff." One called it, "the Russian Declaration of Independence." Another charged the reporter with "using all the Commie tricks, putting God's name on a radical petition." A later effort in New York City by two reporters for the New York *Post* brought nineteen signatures out of one hundred and sixty-one. Only three persons recognized where statements in the petition came from—"nothing but quotations from the Constitution and the Bill of Rights"—and found it "safe" to sign. In an address in Detroit President Truman commented on the frame of mind the Wisconsin endeavor disclosed: "The doubters and defeatists have now taken up another battle cry. They are saying that Americans cannot trust each other. They are trying to stir up trouble between the people and their government. . . . This malicious propaganda has gone so far that on the Fourth of July, over in Madison, Wisconsin, people were afraid to say they believed in the Declaration of Independence."

Such then is the American Idea or the idea of freedom, with its postulation of "the laws of nature and of nature's God" concerning human nature, human relations, and the human enterprise, its definitions of ends and means with respect to the formation and governance of human groups, its propositions concerning the diversity and unalienability of the ends— in sum, concerning its gradient of cultural change.

V. FACT AND FAITH BEHIND THE AMERICAN IDEA

Basic to the Idea was the conviction that mankind are by nature disposed at least as readily to loving-kindness and to justice as to their opposite, and that this disposition was an adequate dynamic for a free and just society. In 1776, John Adams—who with Benjamin Franklin, Robert Livingston and Roger Sherman was of the committee that assigned to Thomas Jefferson the task of drafting the Declaration of Independence—published a twenty-eight-page tract which he entitled *Thoughts on Government.* Therein he pointed out that most governments are founded on fear, a foundation the people of America rejected. Yet since a passion or principle is indispensable ground for government, this could well be, not fear but "the noblest principle and most generous affection of our nature." What else could more fairly "support the noblest and most generous models of government" than a representative republic which is an "empire of laws, not men," whose constitution "introduces knowledge among the people—inspires them with a conscious dignity becoming to free men— makes [them] brave and enterprising—When before the present epoch had three millions of people full power and a fair opportunity to form and establish the wisest and happiest government that human wisdom can contrive?" Years later James Madison reiterates this insight in, I think, No. 55 of the *Federalist,* arguing, "As there is a degree of depravity in mankind which requires a certain degree of circumspection and distrust, so there are other qualities which justify a certain portion of esteem and confidence."

During Adams' presidency relations with post-revolutionary France, not unlike our present ones with post-revolutionary Russia, caused him to revert to the more traditional view of human nature and its government, only to return long after to the American Idea, which his friendly enemy and inimical friend, Thomas Jefferson, held loyally all his life.

The Idea was not, in fact, the illusory utopianism or political subversion its enemies equated it to. The peoples of America at the time of the Revolution numbered from 2,500,000 to 3,000,000. A third, perhaps more, were foreign-born. Their countries of origin were the United Kingdom (Virginia, Maryland, New England were dominantly English), Holland, Sweden, France, Germany. The French were both Huguenots and Romanists; the Germans were Lutherans, Moravians, Dunkers, Schwenkfelders. The Dutch were Calvinists; the Swedes, Lutherans; and the British—the English, the Scottish, the Welsh, the Irish and the Scotch-Irish—were diversely Episcopalians, Congregationalists, Presbyterians, Methodists, Quakers, Romanists, etc. There were also a few Jews. And of course there were the Negroes [1] and the "Redskins," and beyond the

[1] Negroes were imported to the Western Hemisphere because its indigenous peoples, miscalled "Indians," either resisted dehumanization by Europeans into "tools with life in them," or being so reduced, quickly perished, on the *latifundia* of their civilizers, of ill-treatment and disease. Thus, the very great majority of the peoples south of the Rio Grande remain "Indian." Although the speech of the dominant classes is Spanish or Portuguese and the religion Roman Catholic, the native subject multitudes continue as the inheritors and conservators of their ancestral cultures—Mayan, Toltec, Aztec, Inca or other, and continue to digest in these the Iberian speech, manners, creeds, codes, arts and crafts of their Spanish and Portuguese conquerors. For that Iberian culture, especially its common Christianity, claims are often made to the effect that its transplantation to the Americas fulfills a divine purpose, bringing the Indians Christ's salvation to the greater glory of God.

But on the record, it appears to have made but a thin and patchwork patina over the native cultures. The latter, in the course of the centuries have penetrated and suffused it, often violently; while the European stocks themselves have been diminishing, with a slowly mounting momentum, in "purity," prestige, and power. Brazil, indeed, exemplifies the happier, freer formation of this process, for in Brazil, the slave from Africa, the native Indian, and the Portuguese master, mingle both their bloods and lights, and create, more freely than elsewhere in the Americas, a new ethno-cultural community. Nor is this innovative process absent from the rest of the continent. For with the freer trade in knowledge and know-how that the American Idea clearly and distinctly implies and obscurely brings, there came to the native peoples south of the Rio Grande an awakening sense of their equal dignity and worth with the soi-disant master-race from Europe. The awakening has been slow, unsteady, arduous, bloody, often cruel, but it goes on, bringing the Indian the conviction of his equal right, in the fullness of his *Indian* being, to life, liberty and the pursuit of happiness, and therewith the recalling and reinterpretation of his unremembered yet unforgotten past, and the repristination of his cultures for the formation of the Indian's frontier, Spaniards. Their contemporaries in Europe idealized the "Redskins"—vide Voltaire's tale of the noble Huron—as the simple, honest, kindly, intelligent children of nature, the true representatives of Rousseau's natural man with his natural rights. The Europeans in America, with some few exceptions, treated them as enemies by nature, against whom they must

future as Indian in the modern world. In the situation, such a future will be marked by an orchestration with instead of a subordination to the Iberian cultures; the term *Latin-American* will signalize union in equal liberty, of the two members of the hyphen, and denote a genuine cultural pluralism.

However, these observations are a long way from the early decades of the sixteenth century, when the native's forebears, ennobled by the Christian charity of their European conquerors into chattel slaves, were being rapidly done to death on their own soil, which divine mercy gave unto their conquerors for an irrevocable inheritance. Being "savages," baptism was for them an everlasting mercy, and grace enough. But that they should be worked to death, perishing like flies on the latifundia was not grace enough for the holders of the great estates, nor for Father Las Casas, whom the chattels' plight moved to indignation and pity. To him they were not, as to the noble dons, chiefly if not only tools with life in them; and since the plantations must go on, the reverend Father conceived that the Indians should be replaced by substitutes and surrogates. Not white Europeans, God forbid, though the multitudes were in a state of serfdom or slavery: black Africans, rather, whose natural destiny among whites was traditionally chatteldom. Father Las Casas won the consent of both the Pope and the Spanish King and Holy Roman Emperor to this replacement. By 1517 he had persuaded devout Charles the Fifth to grant certain Flemish merchants the right to sell black Africans to white Europeans in the Americas. The transoceanic trade in human flesh thus initiated became a source of enormous profits. Africa had the goods, which needed only to be hunted down, trapped, caged, and transported in Portuguese, Dutch and British bottoms to the Americas.

In both North and South America white wealth was counted with horses, cattle, and land, in so many heads of colored slaves. In North America, the time soon came when imported Negroes outnumbered native Indians. It was practically two centuries before any part of Christendom repudiated slavery and condemned the slave trade. The dehumanization which the sixteenth century paleface priest, out of pity for one group of colored mankind, had let loose upon another, was denounced and forbidden as unchristian by a handful of eighteenth-century Plain People whose Christian initiative was prophetic of the American Idea. They were, indeed, Americans—Pennsylvania Quakers—farmers. Their statement of 1727 was the beginning of the Abolition Movement. Politically, although not culturally, consummated in 1865, the movement has since been gathering a slow momentum toward cultural consummation. But overt traffic in human beings no longer has almost anywhere the sanction of law (Saudi Arabia is the oil-rich exception), and lies under interdict of the law of nations. Of course, practice is still very far from consummating principle, or actuality aspiration; for there is also still no part of the world, "savage" or civilized, genuinely purged of all forms of slavery or peonage.

wage a perennial war of force and fraud, for life and land, although there was more than land enough for everybody, and then for everybody else. To the Europeans "America" meant much the same thing as America now means to Mr. Tucci's Italians. Here is how Jean de Crevecoeur signalizes it in his *Letters From An American Farmer* published in London in 1782:

The rich stay in Europe; it is only the middling and the poor that emigrate. In this great American asylum, the poor of Europe have by some means met together, and in consequence of various Causes: to what purpose should they ask of one another, of what countrymen are they? Alas, two-thirds of them had no country. Can a wretch who works and starves—can that man call England or any other kingdom his country? A country that had no bread for him whose fields procured him no harvest, who met nothing but the frowns of the rich, the severity of the laws, with jails and punishments; who owned not a single foot of the extensive surface of this planet? No. Urged by divers motives, here they came—everything tended to regenerate them; new laws, a new mode of living, a new social system; here they are become men; in Europe they were so many useless plants, wanting vegetable mold and refreshing showers; they were withered and mowed down by want, hunger and war; but now by the power of transplantation, like all other plants they have taken root and flourished! Formerly they were not numbered in any civil list of their country, except in those of the poor; here they rank as citizens. By what invisible power has this surprising metamorphosis been performed? By that of the laws of their industriousness—his country is now that which gives him land, bread, protection and consequence. *Ubi panis, ibi patria* is the motto of all emigrants. Here the rewards of his industry follow with equal steps in the progress of his labor.

As against this working of the American Idea we must, however, set the intention and experience of those who rejected the Idea. It cost them, even more than the believers, immensely in blood, sweat, tears and treasure. Called by the embattled patriots, Tories,[1] and by themselves, Loyalists, they

---

[1] Cf. Thomas Paine, *The American Crisis, II:* "He that is not a supporter of the independent states of America in the same degree that his religious and political principles would suffer him to support the government of any other country, of which he called himself as subject, is, in the American sense of the word, a *Tory;* and the instant that he endeavors to bring his toryism into

were essentially European in spirit and allegiance—European gentlemen in exile. Their education, their manners, their possessions, their dress, diet and houses, their entire culture was English. They identified with the monarchy and shared the fortunes of its troops. When these were at last defeated, they also, sixty thousand strong, left the country as Colonials returning to the motherland. Their disaster was perhaps far greater than that with which those whose fighting faith was the American Idea paid for their faith.

VI. THE AMERICAN IDEA IN THE CONSTITUTION: THE GREAT SEAL AND THE FLAG

The winning of Independence was followed by the multitude of uncertainties of domestic bankruptcy and foreign exploitation; by the States' threats to revert to warring sovereignties at home, by the cold wars and the several hot wars waged by foreign foes. One included the capture and burning of Washington. Nevertheless, the thirteen colonies that had confederated to fight a common war for their thirteen independencies and then turned away from each other, did somehow orchestrate their competing diversities in the light of the American Idea, and did shape them toward "a more perfect union" wherewith they could "establish justice, insure domestic tranquillity, provide for the common defence, promote the general welfare, and secure the blessings of liberty to [themselves] and their posterity."

In this endeavor, the framing and adoption of the Constitution was a reaction to imminent anarchy; the adoption of the Bill of Rights a reaction to the Constitution's potentiality of tyranny. Awareness of the fact of difference, of the parity of differences, not political merely, but also ethno-cultural and religious, exerted on both a cybernetic influence. This the Great Seal and the flag of the United States both exemplify.

---

practice, he becomes a *Traitor*. The first can only be detected by a general test, and the law hath already provided for the latter."

Conversely, tory Dr. Samuel Johnson stigmatized the Americans who called themselves Patriots as a "race of convicts who ought to be thankful for anything we allow them, short of hanging." They were, he said, "Rascals, Robbers, Pirates." He could love every other variety of mankind but not Americans. The bearing of these contrasted expressions on both left and right totalitarianism in today's United States does not need to be pointed up.

The Seal presently used—anyone who has a dollar bill can see both sides of it on the greenback—bears on the obverse, the eagle with thirteen arrows in its claws, on the reverse, the altar-like thirteen-step pyramid capped by "the eye of Providence in a radiant triangle," with the motto, *ANNUIT COEPTIS* above, and *NOVUS ORDO SECLORUM* below. But the first form was more complex and was intended to express the ethno-cultural as well as the political configuration of our Republic. The Committee whom John Hancock named on July 4, 1776, to devise the Great Seal consisted of three of the men who brought in the Declaration of Independence —Thomas Jefferson, John Adams, Benjamin Franklin. On August 10th Jefferson reported for the Committee. They had canvassed and appraised the multitude of suggestions sent them and composed the latters' diversity into a design. They proposed that the seal should be engraved on the obverse with a shield divided into six quarterings, symbolizing the six major lands of origin of the American people—England, Scotland, Ireland, France, Germany, Holland; there should also be one escutcheon each for each of the thirteen colonies; the right hand support should be the Goddess of Liberty; the left hand, the Goddess of Justice; a crest at the top should contain the eye of Providence in radiant triangle. The motto was to be: E Pluribus Unum. The engraving on the reverse was to show tyrant Pharaoh in an open Chariot amid the waters of the Red Sea. By the seal finally adopted only federal strength (the Eagle with the Arrows) and political union (the pyramid under the divine eye) are symbolized. The Latin expressions *Annuit Coeptis, Novus Ordo Seclorum* affirm the enduring conviction of the founding fathers and their successors that this "new nation, conceived in liberty and dedicated to the proposition that all men are created equal" was the beginning of a "new order of the ages," an order which establishes and fulfils the intent of *e pluribus unum*. This is also the primal signification of the Stars and Stripes.

VII. AMERICANISM AS A CULTURE

In the United States conscious change along the gradient laid down by the Declaration, by the Preamble and the Amendments to the Constitution was and continues to be an

Americanization of pre-American and un-American culture complexes.[1] To no small degree it is the same abroad. The change consists of the labors of men and women everywhere,

[1] Many writers argue that the establishment of a free union of the diverse was the aim of the Federalist Party. The record suggests, however, that this party, whose spokesman was Alexander Hamilton, was seeking a political structure more traditional. Its ideal has been qualified as "nationalism" and set over against the "federalism" of the Republican—later the Democratic—Party, whose leader and prophet was Thomas Jefferson. On the record the *Federalists* pursued ends with a certain affinity to the centralized government without the consent of the governed which the Declaration repudiated and the Constitution was designed to render impossible. Certainly, such Federalists as George Washington, John Adams, his son, John Quincy, and John Marshall, were in principle constitutional nationalists. But no less such were Thomas Jefferson, James Madison, James Monroe and Andrew Jackson. The practice of the former, however, tended to go beyond their constitutional principles, and the practice of the latter tended to minimize their federalist assumptions. The latter implemented *union* in order to insure equal liberty for individuals against both federal power and "state-rights"; the former implemented *union* in order to overrule both individual rights and state sovereignties on behalf of centralized and unresponsive, if not irresponsible, governmental power; they thus clashed with the Bill of Rights. As I read the record, the Bill of Rights was the crux of the issue between the Federalists and the Republicans. The one would have such coercive "law and order" as would sell liberty for security; the other was concerned for a "law and order" as would provide security for liberty.

Those so disposed might attibute to the favor of a benevolent providence the fact that during the administrations of Jefferson, Madison, Monroe and Jackson, judicial decisions as to the scope and meaning of constitutional law were made predominantly by John Marshall, a Federalist by party affiliation, but a constitutional nationalist by conviction. One may greatly doubt whether any of the Republican presidents would have dissented from that Chief Justice's own statement of his nationalist faith, when he wrote: "In heart and sentiment, as well as by birth and interest, I am an American, attached to the genuine principles of the Constitution, as sanctioned by the will of the people, for their general liberty, prosperity and happiness. I consider that Constitution as the rock of our political salvation, which has preserved us from misery, division and civil wars; and which will yet preserve us if we value it rightly and support it firmly."

It is possible, but not easy, to disagree with the opinion that John Marshall's interpretation of the Constitution enabled the loose and precarious union of independent and sovereign states with diverse and conflicting traditions of individual liberty to become the vital inward means of rendering this liberty everywhere secure. The vital momentum, the dynamic togetherness for which he devised gradients, became thus adequate to overcome the civil war, the misery and the division which nevertheless Americans inflicted on one another. All the latter can be very reasonably credited to infirm support and false valuations of the Constitution by factions which—James Madison warned of them in the tenth paper of *The Federalist*—schemed to subordinate to their factional interest all the people's "general liberty, prosperity and happiness."

who had taken the American Idea for their saving faith, to reshape the ideals, customs, and traditions of their societies in harmony with this Idea, much as the hellenization of classical antiquity consisted in endeavors to reshape ancient societies into configurations consonant with the Athenian Idea. Americanization early suggested "not a race but an intelligence," and came to denote the culture of all whose credo is the American Idea, whatever their blood. Indeed, any reader of the *Federalist* knows this; anyone aware of the intellectual history of such founding fathers as Jefferson, Adams, Franklin, Madison, Marshall, Monroe, Wythe, Randolph is aware of this; anyone knows this who knows how much the literature of the Roman Republic fed their conception of the American one, and how in their deliberations, the sense of the frontier without a past and of the past without a frontier had consequences in their pattern of government for a free society of free men.

This pattern brought something new into the world because it transvalued liberty from a hereditary privilege of a select few, whose freedom was postulated on the enslavement of the many, into the inalienable right of all the many, and endowed that right with power to make itself respected by the political device of representative government. This device, in the opinion of Thomas Paine (*The Rights of Man—Part II*) "is the invention of the modern world." It is the one effective alternative to hereditary government which "has not the right to exist." When "we take from any man the exercise of hereditary powers we take away that which he never had the right to possess, and which no law or custom could, or ever can, give him a title to." The feeling of the world-wide import of the American Creed and Code early became a religious mystique. The wars waged against them have been religious wars, at home and abroad. It was a mystique of freedom whose rites are reason, theoretical and practical. Quaker Thomas Paine was by no means a lonely voice of the faith, but he was the most devout, the most lucid and the most enduring and long-suffering. To him *America* became the word made flesh and walking on earth. His *Rights of Man* speaks that enfleshed word. Its intent is to vindicate the American Idea as faith and as works against the attack on it, in form of a critique of the French Revolution by a sage spokesman for the vested interests of tradition, Edmund Burke.

The independence of America [Paine wrote in the Introduction to Part II] considered merely as a separation from England, would have been a matter of but little importance, had it not been accompanied by a revolution in the principles and practices of governments. She made a stand, not for herself only, but for the world, and looked beyond the advantages herself could receive. Even the Hessian, though hired to fight against her, may live to bless his defeat; and England, condemning the viciousness of its government, rejoice in its miscarriage.

As America was the only spot in the political world where the principle of universal reformation could begin, so also was it the best in the natural world. An assemblage of circumstances conspired, not only to give birth, but to add gigantic maturity to its principles. The scene which that country presents to the eye of a spectator, has something in it which generates and encourages great ideas. Nature appears to him in magnitude. The mighty objects he beholds act upon his mind by enlarging it, and he partakes of the greatness he contemplates. Its first settlers were immigrants from different European nations, and of diversified professions of religion, retiring from the governmental persecutions of the old world, and meeting in the new, not as enemies, but as brothers. The wants which necessarily accompany the cultivation of a wilderness produced among them a state of society, which countries long harassed by the quarrels and intrigues of governments, had neglected to cherish. In such a situation man becomes what he ought. He sees his species, not with the inhuman idea of a natural enemy, but as kindred; and the example shews to the artificial world that man must go back to Nature for information.

VIII. THE ROLE OF THE FRONTIER

Long before the historian Turner used it as a principle of explanation to account for the American character, the impact of wilderness and frontier was a vivid fact in the mind of Paine, and less explicitly, in the minds of Jefferson and Franklin.[1] The "winning of the West" was in effect an accul-

---

[1] Franklin: "I have some little property in America. I will freely spend nineteen shillings in the pound to defend the right of refusing the other shilling; and, after all, if I cannot defend that right, I can retire cheerfully with my little family into the boundless woods of America, which are sure to furnish freedom and subsistence to any man who can bait a hook or pull a trigger."

turation of the European to the cultural economy of the American Indian and a concomitant deculturation from the cultural economy of the peoples of Europe. The first Americanization of Europeans was Indianization, an alteration of diet, dress, shelter, healing, perceptions, skills and values. Rank, prestige, leadership, knowledge and know-how became functions of their efficacy as organs of survival; their values were set by their relevancy and use; ancestry, learning, all deference to the past, as intrinsically authoritative and reverend, gave way to appraisals of its bearing on the future, on its consequence to survival and development. The rites and ceremonies of assembly and communication, the elaborations and refinements of speech, dress and manners, the entire fat of culture were slowly worn, sometimes swiftly stripped, down to working, fighting form. The drama of the Admirable Crichton symbolizes the reversal; only, in the play, Europeanism is restored; in American history there is a perennial struggle to restore it, which as perennially fails—so far. An American idiom tells the tale. It is *make good*. It implies that values accrue to persons and institutions by achievement, not inheritance. It implies that the conditions of achievement are equal liberty not only for individuals as such but also for their societies and institutions. Their religions, their businesses, all their enterprises, must *make good* in undertakings each of which carries its own hazard, none of which has its success guaranteed as of right in advance. Whether by inherited or delegated authority, all are free enterprises. If they are competing with one another, then the success consists in doing the same job better than their competitors, and whatever be the field, "better" is a first and last decision of the believer or consumer, not the claim of the undertaker.

As Jefferson had already written regarding freedom of religion in October of 1776:

From the dissention among the sects arises necessarily a right of chusing, a necessity of deliberation, to which we will conform. But if we chuse for ourselves, we must allow others to chuse also, and so reciprocally, this establishes religious liberty.

The first freedom is the freedom of choice, and its first field cannot be anything other than the inward field of belief and

thought and expression. Free enterprise for the mind is the ineluctable precondition of every other variety of free enterprise. What follows from it in religion indicates its consequence
in every other institution of a cultural economy. Laws assuring it, such as Jefferson's Statute of Religious Liberty for his
"country," Virginia, are denounced, by spokesmen for vested
interests in keeping minds bound, as "irreligious," "atheistic,"
etc., etc. Yet, also such religious Toryism has enjoyed a degree
of security, growth and prosperity under such laws, and all
cults and denominations have found ways of freely and peacefully living and working together, unprecedented in the war
of the faiths which marks the long history of Judaeo-Christian-
ism. The trend is signalized by today's "interfaith" enterprises
at home and abroad, and can be observed in other formations
of the cultural economy, such as the familial, the educational,
the hygienic, the economic and the political. There, also, the
function of the laws remains "to render unto everyone his
right"; according to the intent of the American Idea, to keep
the ways of life equally open to the enterprise of whoever in
good faith freely chooses to seek his spiritual or material fortune upon them, venturing on his own power at his own risk.
The people resulting, even in the eyes of so critical and
plangent an observer as George Santayana, is a people marked
by "much forgetfulness, much callow disrespect for what is
past or alien; but there is a fund of vigour, goodness, and hope
such as no nation ever possessed before. In what sometimes
looks like American greediness and jostling for the front place,
all is love of achievement, nothing is unkindness; it is a fear-
less people and free from malice, as you might see in their
eyes and gestures, even if their conduct did not prove it."
And one may add, the waves of mccarthyism notwithstanding, these are still the distinctive traits of the "typical" American and of the American mind.

Of course, that laws are required, evidences the enduring
depth and range of the antagonisms which the American Idea
faces and the strength and variety of the barriers it must ever-
lastingly level, in order to keep the ways equally open. Once
an In-group has achieved a certain pattern of stability, its
attitude toward any influence that might alter this inner balance becomes suspicious and unfriendly. A xenophobia de-

velops and creeds and codes are projected which rationalize
it. These are the signature of a spiritual stasis wherein the conservation and repetition of a past unchanged becomes all the
future its *aficionados* desire.

At the frontier, however, survival depends on mobility, on
a certain readiness and free functioning of the mind, vigilant
to appraise the unexpected and to bet, with some prejudgment
of the consequence of alternative actions, on one of them for
achievement or survival. Resulting was a certain indifference
to any man's past; an acceptance, instead, of his perceptual
singularity as a prophecy of his future role. Men's credentials
were in their immediate presence, their face value, and they
confirmed it by actual performance; who they were, whence
they came, were irrelevancies; they were whatever they appeared to be; and only how they did could establish whether
the appearance was false. The cliché, "wide open spaces where
men are men," signified a genuine experience, before it became an artificial sentimentality. There were, of course, narrow, closed spaces as well; but in the latter, men could at best
only endure; while the former liberated their powers and
called forth their manhood, eliciting will and vigilance and
developing skill to *make good.*

Goethe, in his distant Weimar, perceived with his poet's eye
what these Americans were living out with heart and reins,
betting their future on the American Idea. He wrote in 1827:

> *Amerika, du hast es besser*
> *Als unser Kontinent, das alte;*
> *Du hast keine verfallene Schlosser*
> *Und keine Basalte.*
>
> *Dich stört nicht im Innern*
> *Zum lebendigen Zeit*
> *Unnutzes Errinern*
> *Und vergebliche Streit.*
>
> *Benutzt die Gegenwart mit Glück*
> *Und wenn nur euere Kinder dichten*
> *Bewahre sie ein gut' Geschick,*
> *Vor Ritter, Rauber, und Gespenstergesichten.*

IX. THE HUMAN FRONTIERS

In due course, the frontiers of the continental wilderness were replaced by frontiers of settled communions. One, set up by European whites long before the American Idea, was the frontier of color—the frontier against native Indians, African Negroes, and other "coloreds." The "winning of the West" became a war of exploitation and extermination against the Indians, in the course of which they were transvalued, from the idealized natural man many of whose qualities and culture it would be—and many a time was—salvation to emulate, into a dirty, ruthless, cruel savage who had no rights any "white man" need respect. Wherever subdued, the Indian was made the ward of the Great White Father in Washington, and kept in a state of artificial inferiority, his culture treated as "savage," his rights to equal education and freedom of enterprise with whites unconceded or exploited. A book discussing this treatment is entitled *A Century of Dishonor*. Only long after the turn of the new century was the Indian's cultural economy seen and interpreted in the frame of reference of the American Idea and a new program devised which envisaged his cultural survival and growth as a different and equal fellow citizen amid the diverse formations of white enterprise. The program is always precarious and its implementation regularly obstructed by rapacious whites greedy to possess and exploit the natural resources of Indian Reservations, notably oil. There has been, among certain persons of—if not good will—at least not ill will, ironically curious talk about "Americanization" for the American Indian. An Association on American Indian Affairs, with some kinship of faith and works to the Abolitionists of an earlier day, argues per contra for "the right to be Indian," and for the inalienable right of Indians to decide for themselves how they will exercise their unalienable rights to life, liberty and the pursuit of happiness.

The breaching of the frontier against the Negro has a different, better known, no less bloody and dramatic story. It was recognized and felt from the beginning that the American Idea and the institution of slavery could never be reconciled. The penalization of a human being because his skin is dark, and the employment of religion, philosophy, and science to justify this imposition on a human being of the character and role of a tool with life in it, of a property to be bought and sold like any other possession, was from the very start recognized as a rapacious blasphemy against "the laws of nature and of nature's God." From 1789 to 1861, the issue was joined in debate, in legislation, in bloody confrontations on the soil of "bleeding Kansas," on the streets of Boston, at Harpers Ferry, and many other places. "Abolitionism" was an issue that suffused and slanted all other issues.[1] The Union of States might have been broken on it; and if "the North" had been defeated in the Civil War which was fought over it, the Union would have been broken. But the North won the War. The white men who fought in the Northern armies were free men. So were the white men who fought in the Southern armies. But the Southerners were free men fighting to keep in slavery other men on whose bondage their own freedom fed. The Negroes in the Northern armies were freed men or slaves, fighting to win and hold freedom for themselves. The white men in the Northern armies were free men fighting for the equal liberty of other men in most ways different from themselves, and kept as chattel slaves by other white men simply because they were black and not white. I know of no parallel to this in any war anywhere that history records. History records wars of slaves to free themselves, wars of free men to preserve their freedom, and of course plenty of wars by free men to destroy other men's freedom. But nowhere is there a

---

[1] Hear James Russell Lowell:

> "Is true freedom but to break
> Fetters for our own dear sake,
> And with leathern hearts forget
> That we owe mankind a debt?
> No; true freedom is to share,
> All the chains our brothers wear,
>   And, with heart and hand, to be
>   Earnest to make others free.

> "They are slaves who fear to speak
> For the fallen and the weak;
> They are slaves who will not choose
> Hatred, scoffing, and abuse,
> Rather than in silence shrink
> From the truth they needs must think;
>   They are slaves who dare not be
>   In the right with two or three."

record of a war waged by free men with the fighting faith in equal liberty which is the American Idea, to set unfree men free. In this, the Civil War between the States is unique.[1]

Its first lasting consequence was to vindicate the principle of the dynamic interdependence between the Federal Union and the equal right of every individual to his personal liberty: we recall Webster's famous phrase, *Liberty and Union, one and inseparable, now and forever*. It had been no easy thing to pass from the wartime alliance of thirteen independent and sovereign states which, by the Articles of Confederation, contracted to fight together in a common rebellion against a common overlord, through a reversion to competitive and on occasion embattled sovereignties, to the Federal Union established and ordained by the Constitution of the United States. "Rights reserved to the States" long meant the exclusive control of a state's domestic affairs by that state's government: its sovereign right to regulate human relations, religion, education, military affairs, the arts and the sciences. Many long assumed that state rights meant the subjection of the individual citizen to every rule of his state government. Spokesmen for the South, endeavoring to vindicate the institution of slavery, invoked States' Rights. There is currently such an invocation against the Supreme Court's unanimous decision that segregation in the schools is unconstitutional. Inasmuch as an individual American who suffers wrong or oppression at the hands of a state government has no alternative to force and violence other than recourse for justice to the Federal Government, this becomes by custom and tradition the conservator and defender of his equal liberty; Union and Liberty are recognized as members of one another. Per contra, the idea of State Rights falls from its libertarian initiation to the level of an instrument serving anti-libertarian ends. Save for certain cases of extradition, there has occurred, during the half century, hardly any appeal to State Rights which was not an appeal on behalf of some special privilege or exclusive advantage such as racial segregation, offshore oil, electric power monopoly, or the re-

[1] Cf. Walt Whitman regarding this war: "Probably no future age can know, but I well know, how the gist of this fiercest and most resolute of the world's warlike contentions resided exclusively in the unnamed, unknown, rank and file; how the brunt of its labor of death, to all essential purposes, was volunteered. The people, of their own choice, fighting, dying, for their own idea."

placement of Federal by States' jurisdiction over Indians within their borders (Public Law 2801).

Nevertheless, State Rights neither need nor should be inimical to the upkeep of a free cultural economy. If they are all too often resorted to for ends unfriendly to equal liberty, they also enable and assure regional diversities in culture. Differences of scene and setting, of temperament, of tempo, of perception, speech, and other modes of relating people and handling tools and things, attain, in the context of States' Rights, a certain configuration and group personality which may engage in a strengthening and fructifying interstate commerce in cultural values. Especially important to the pluralism on which a vital culture thrives are the right and opportunity to initiate local experiments whose methods, patterns and result may then become objects of study, imitation and emulation, even as modes of dress and fashions in literature, music and the arts are for individuals. States, too, have their Joneses to keep up with. The Congress, for example, was prevented by certain vested State interests from adopting a law regarding Fair Employment Practices. But the legislature of the State of New York did pass one, and thus set up a standard that soon or late other states would emulate.

The task of insuring the equal rights of the different to work on equal terms, is involved with the second lasting consequence of the Civil War: the addition of the 13th, 14th and 15th Amendments of the Constitution to the nation's fundamental law. From whatever causes, "reconstruction" failed. The Negro Americans of the South in due course found themselves with rights under the law, and neither the power, nor the knowledge which is power, to make good those rights. The white Americans of the region translated their pre-war past into a culture to mourn for and an idol to appeal to. They dedicated their present, far less to building a new cultural economy, nor even so far as they might, rebuilding the old one, than to keeping from their Negro fellow citizens the equality won for them at such cost of blood and treasure and guaranteed to them by the laws. Their end was "white supremacy" and their end justified their means. End and means found symbolic incarnation in the Ku Klux Klan.

During nearly the century since the close of the Civil War,

the Americanization of the light and dark Americans of the South, the acculturation of their powers and passions to the American Idea, has been a slow, wasteful and arduous process. In the course of it, the Negro's music, sacred and secular, his dances, his legends and folklore, his group's epics and his personal histories have flowed into the stream of the arts and letters of American culture and enriched it with the singularities of the authentic Negro difference. Somewhat it has done so by the works of white sympathizers, admirers and borrowers; mostly it has been the autogenous expression of the Negro "racial minority" itself, as its members achieved the power of self-help through the activities of self-education, and thereafter worked spontaneous expression over into conscious art. The Negro American's way to the America of the American Idea is still long, long, but he is on the way; and who has the will to stay him has not the power; who has the power has not the will.[1]

So, also is the Southern White upon the way, less desirously, perhaps less needfully, as long as he remains a self-isolating Southerner maintaining "white supremacy" by keeping the Negro down, instead of justifying and demonstrating it by lifting himself up in equal competition. But his spokesmen now call attention to a "new South" and this is not the South of "the man Bilbo" or of the one-time Secretary of State, Associate Justice of the Supreme Court, Director of the Office of Social Security, who was lately governor of the Sovereign State of South Carolina. This is the South that was once the South of Thomas Jefferson and James Madison and George Washington, and is now the South of Frank Graham, of Lillian Smith, of William Faulkner, of all the generation in whose hearts and heads the American Idea renews its life.

X. THE AMERICAN IDEA AND THE NEW RACISM

For the North's frontiersmen of the spirit, fighting the Civil War was an act of religion, the moment of truth in their commitment to the American Idea. But quick upon the letdown which naturally came after that high engagement, fol-

---

[1] See Booker T. Washington: *Up from Slavery*; Alain Locke: *The New Negro; Pluralism and Ideological Peace* (in "Freedom and Experience," Sidney Hook and Milton Konvitz, editors).

lowed the abortions of Reconstruction, the insurgence of a diversity of busy entrepreneurs, cutthroat go-getters who are favorably remembered as captains of industry, railway princes, oil magnates, iron dukes, copper, cotton or cattle kings, unfavorably as robber barons. Their enterprises, Thorstein Veblen suggests, were postulated on getting something for nothing, by legitimate or legally authorized illegitimate right, and if not that, on getting the most for the least. Their raiding of the public lands is well known, much discussed; their seduction and exploitation of the peasantries of Europe, less so. The America of the American Idea was a natural lure to bring these peasantries to the America of un-American project and practice. Free immigration brought on the miscellany of Europe to serve as the hewers of wood and drawers of water of us "who built America." With the strength of their bodies and the skills of their hands came also their unlettered diversities of speech, dress, diet, creed, and worship; their habits of submission to authority and of deference to apparent power. Even the rebels among them were uninstructed and unpracticed in the ways of free societies and the procedures of democracies. Their culture was authoritarian, its ideas were totalitarian.

The combination of untoward developments—of reconstruction perverted, of free enterprise become piratical, of concurrent mass immigration of peoples conspicuously different—produced, in many sensitive and thoughtful veterans and their younger relatives and friends, a not unfamiliar disillusion and anxiety. An earlier reaction to immigrant otherness had been a suspicious, somewhat disgusted, nativism. Even the wholly libertarian Henry Thoreau made public his vigorous distaste for the "shanty Irish" newly settled in his New England. The alarmed anxieties of S. F. B. Morse, whose warnings regarding the intentions for America of Europe's Holy Alliance had started off American Knownothingism, were not due to immigration as such but to its use by European autocracy to infiltrate the national life with authoritarian, sacerdotal religion for the subversion of the American Idea.

To Charles Eliot Norton the changes ensuing upon the Civil War were a perversion of the Idea, an abandonment of the quest for diversity in experience, the encounter with one another of traditions and convictions, in thought, and the coming in their place of the pursuit of what William James came to call "the bitch-goddess, success." Norton saw America falling to that barbarous leveling materialism that Mark Twain disclosed in *The Gilded Age*. Others in their disillusion sought safety and controlled order in the American variant of the Church of England; still others in the American arm of the Church of Rome. The churchly pretensions to doctrinal invariancy and ritual stability seemed a refuge from the insecure openness of the free religious conscience whose voices had been Emerson, Theodore Parker, even Walt Whitman. Still others, Norton among them, found a safe retreat in cut-flower culture—in the literature and the arts of Europe, reverenced, discriminated, and savored without regard to their causes or consequences. This, in due course, became also a passing concern of Henry James. An aestheticism, looking mostly to the Gothic, took its competitive stand alongside the sacerdotalism. As Henry Adams viewed and interpreted them, Mont Saint Michel and Chartres had expressed an organic wholeness from which all human events have ever since been a dispersion. Now the Dynamo had dethroned the Virgin, and the Second Law of Thermodynamics was impelling "the democratic dogma" to an ever-accelerating "degradation" whose *terminus ad quem* must needs be utter collapse and nullity.

A new sort of racism emerged to segregate and account for the American past and to rationalize present claims. This has its analogies with the racism of Kipling's "white man's burden." But it was not a racism of color as in imperial Britain and America's Southern states. It was a racism of culture. It claimed that the American Idea and the American Way were hereditary to the Anglo-Saxon stock and to that stock only; that other stocks were incapable of producing them, learning them and living them. If, then, America is to survive as a culture of creed and code, it can do so only so long as the chosen Anglo-Saxon race retains its integrity of flesh and spirit and freely sustains and defends their American expression against alien contamination. Universal suffrage, for example, *is* such a contamination. To entrust alien settlers with the power of the ballot was to arm them with a weapon that could wound and kill. The refugees taking up their habitations in the land that so many true believers in the American Idea—from Thomas Paine to Theodore Parker—had signalized as "the asylum of humanity" were threatening to wreck their asylum.

On another level, this anxious segregative racist sentiment brought into being such companies as The Daughters of the American Revolution, The Sons of the American Revolution, the Daughters of the Confederacy, and others. To qualify for initiation into these companies, the postulant must provide satisfactory proof that she or he has at least one revolutionary or confederate ancestor. There is also a company of Colonial Dames whose ancestors must be pre-Revolutionary and may be Tory. But the invidious distinction of birth is not enough; to it are joined distinctions of color and faith; a commitment against immigration and for isolation, and programs of study of American history on the basis of assumptions that would render the American Idea a subversive force in the national enterprise. Their assumptions make the word "patriot" mean today what "loyalist" or Tory meant during the Revolution, and "disloyal," "subversive," what "patriot" then meant.

So, together with Ku Klux Klan and other "patriotic" societies, a would-be American hereditary aristocracy consciously shape themselves. They are, of course, to be appraised against another aristocracy which the American Way has unconsciously formed and consciously acknowledged. This, somewhat in the spirit of Jefferson and Condorcet, is an aristocracy of education. It is signalized by the expression "college man." The expression confers a differential status not unlike that conferred by a genealogical tree, and maintained with as little reference to the superior status conferred by wealth or privilege.

Daughters, Sons, Klans, Dames, are obviously In-groups who feel and resent the challenge of their frontiers not by what the Out-groups *are* but by what they *do*. If they recognize little or no merit in themselves, they call up the merit of the Fathers. They become blind and passionate Xenophobiacs. They are essentially snobs who equate inner difference to outer inequality. They develop formations that would, to themselves, at least, insure and justify the superiority they can perhaps no longer sustain by their knowledge and skill. They attribute to the Outsiders all the evils and misfortunes that happen in their communities and in the national life. They become agitators for restrictive immigration and selecting immigrants in accord with their desires and prejudgments. The change of mood and attitude is signalized by the difference between Emma Lazarus' "New Colossus," which she wrote in 1883, to aid the Bartholdi Pedestal Fund, and Thomas Bailey Aldrich's "Unguarded Gates," which he published in the *Atlantic Monthly* for April, 1892:

Wrote Emma Lazarus:

> Not like the brazen giant of Greek fame,
> With conquering limbs astride from land to land;
> Here at our sea-washed, sunset gates shall stand
> A mighty woman with a torch, whose flame
> Is the imprisoned lightning, and her name
> Mother of Exiles. From her beacon-hand
> Glows world-wide welcome; her mild eyes command
> The air-bridged harbor that twin cities frame.
> "Keep, ancient lands, your storied pomp!" cries she
> With silent lips. "Give me your tired, your poor,
> Your huddled masses yearning to breathe free,
> The wretched refuse of your teeming shore.
> Send these, the homeless, tempest-tost to me,
> I lift my lamp beside the golden door!"

Whereas Mr. Aldrich wrote:

> Wide open and unguarded stand our gates,
> Named of the four winds, North, South, East, and West;
> Portals that lead to an enchanted land
> Of cities, forests, fields of living gold,
> Vast prairies, lordly summits touched with snow,
> Majestic rivers sweeping proudly past,
> The Arab's date-palm and the Norseman's pine—
> A realm wherein are fruits of every zone,
> Airs of all climes, for lo! throughout the year
> The red rose blossoms somewhere—a rich land,
> A later Eden planted in the wilds,
> With not an inch of earth within its bound
> But if a slave's foot press it sets him free!
> Here, it is written, Toil shall have its wage,
> And Honor honor, and the humblest man
> Stand level with the highest in the law.
> Of such a land have men in dungeons dreamed,

And with the vision brightening in their eyes
Gone smiling to the fagot and the sword.

Wide open and unguarded stand our gates,
And through them presses a wild motley throng—
Men from the Volga and the Tartar steppes,
Featureless figures of the Hoang-Ho,
Malayan, Scythian, Teuton, Kelt, and Slav,
Flying the Old World's poverty and scorn;
These bringing with them unknown gods and rites,
Those, tiger passions, here to stretch their claws.
In street and alley what strange tongues are these,
Accents of menace alien to our air,
Voices that once the Tower of Babel knew!
O Liberty, white Goddess! is it well
To leave the gates unguarded? On thy breast
Fold Sorrow's children, soothe the hurts of hate.
Lift the down-trodden, but with hand of steel
Stay those who to thy sacred portals come
To waste the gifts of freedom. Have a care
Lest from thy brow the clustered stars be torn
And trampled in the dust. For so of old
The thronging Goth and Vandal trampled Rome,
And where the temples of the Caesars stood
The lean wolf unmolested made her lair.

There may be some indication of the workings of the American Idea in the fact that "Unguarded Gates" is hardly remembered, even though the anxiety it expresses continues and is currently intense.

XI. THE CONFLICTING "AMERICANIZATIONS"

Now, however superiority be vindicated, it can never feel secure.

In the degree that this "nativist" superiority is acknowledged and accepted, it is emulated. Both an unconscious and a conscious process of acculturation ensues, that generates moral and cultural paradoxes. The usual word for this acculturation is Americanization. From one point of view any immigrant on whom difference from the natives lays a burden of inferiority will take Americanization for identification, for digesting differences from them into sameness with them. From this point of view equality *is* identity, and identity is having become as good as one's soi-disant betters. But if everyone is equally good, and none is better, what becomes of racial election, of hereditary superiority? The superiors cannot easily permit their inferiors to attain their own levels, and to change group status from Outsider to Insider. As they see it, however, Americanization [1] must needs consist first and last of assent to their claims of superiority, and of unemulative willing and obedient conformation to their requirements as betters in all the dimensions of the common life—civil, industrial, religious, aesthetic, intellectual. Anything else is considered "unAmerican," "foreign," "delinquent," "criminal," "socialist," "Communist," "atheist," a heresy imported, not a home-revealed truth. It is signalized as pertaining to a "minority" with whose members free communication would be somehow degradation. The in-group tends toward a Monadism resembling that of a religious order which withdraws from the world and shuts it out, or a church which excommunicates difference as difference, ordaining that there shall be neither worship, nor marriage, nor burial nor eating and drinking with the different on equal terms; stigmatizing disregard of its ordinances as mortal sin and disobedience of God's will.

Obedience, however, renders the churchly taboos and prescriptions powers of communal segregation and isolation. They obstruct, and may even permanently prevent, that free and friendly intercommunication between different communities and their individual communicants wherein the oneness of a free society of diverse equals lives and grows. An obedient communicant is an isolated and segregated communicant; he cannot at the same time be a patriot of the American Idea. To be the latter, he must, as a faithful of his own community, maintain friendship and free communication with the faithful of other communities; he must, in every field of thought and action, make good as a good neighbor, alike in *propria persona* and by means of his communal institutions.

XII. THE FORMATION OF THE BIBLE OF AMERICA

This, if nothing else, is the intent of the American Idea. It starts with the individual. It affirms what Santayana also knew,

[1] The Sons of the American Revolution used to distribute pamphlets of "Information for Immigrants" in a dozen different languages.

that "the individual is the only seat and focus of social forces; [that] if society and government are to be justified at all, they must be justified in his eyes and by his instincts." Hence, the Idea lays the responsibility for his own freedom on the individual's will and courage, designating all association as voluntary, and postulating it on the individual's concern for his own integrity and on his consequent free movement between and among the diversity of group formations. By and large, this intent so far successfully realizes itself in the formation of the national culture *in et e pluribus*. As a creed covenanted by all religions for the freedom of each, the Gospel of America receives, each generation, a fresh philosophical restatement, addressed to the exigencies of the times. As a plan of human relations in the human enterprise, it receives like repristination from the utterances of poets, statesmen, dramatists, men of letters. A sequence of such renewals makes up the Bible of the people of Israel, and of their Christian epigons. In the same way, a selected sequence may make up a Bible of America. Its book of Genesis would of course be the Declaration of Independence, which is also the simplest, clearest, most comprehensive, yet briefest telling of the American Idea. It sets the theme and whatever follows is a variation upon it.

From what follows might be selected George Washington's letter to the Jewish Congregation at Newport; Jefferson's First and Second Inaugurals; his Virginia Bill of Religious Liberty; his letters to John Adams on Natural Aristocracy; certain articles from the *Federalist;* the Constitution; certain decisions and statements of John Marshall's. The Bible might include James Madison's "Memorial and Remonstrance"; James Monroe's promulgation of the Monroe Doctrine; the Constitution of the American Anti-Slavery Society, Horace Mann's Twelfth Report to the Massachusetts Board of Education; the Seneca Falls Declaration on Women's Rights; Abraham Lincoln's "House Divided" Speech; John Brown's speech to the Court that sentenced him; Lincoln's First and Second Inaugurals, his Gettysburg Address and his Emancipation Proclamation; the Preamble to the Constitution of the Noble Order of the Knights of Labor; Woodrow Wilson's First Inaugural, his Address to the Congress on War Aims and Peace Terms, his statement on the League of Nations; certain dissenting opinions of Messrs. Holmes and Brandeis; Bartolomeo Vanzetti's Last Statement to the Court, and H. M. Kallen's "The Two Anarchisms"; the Kellogg Peace Pact, various addresses of President Franklin Roosevelt's, especially that on the Four Freedoms; President Truman's message to Congress defining the Truman Doctrine; the Reports of his Commission on Higher Education and on Civil Rights; certain decisions of the Supreme Court regarding separation of Church and State, and Racial Discrimination. And the Bible might conclude its unfinished political Torah with the Universal Declaration of Human Rights adopted by the Assembly of the United Nations.

Its books of prophets and scriptures would be drawn from poetic repristinations of the American Idea. Selections might be made from the prose and verse of Emerson, of Whittier and Lowell, of Walt Whitman—especially of Walt Whitman, of Herman Melville, of Mark Twain, of Henry James, of Vachel Lindsay, of Robert Frost, of Carl Sandburg and others. And the Idea's philosophic renewal would be represented by essays of Thomas Paine, Ralph Waldo Emerson, Henry Thoreau, Josiah Royce, William James, John Dewey. These American philosophers' image of the human person signalizes his irreducible individuality. They see it as free, friendly, energetic, venturesome, looking only for a free field and no favors, ready to bet its powers and possessions on undertakings whose success is not and cannot be guaranteed in advance.

The metaphysical perspectives in which they set this constellated image are diverse and in many ways incommensurable.

Paine was a Quaker, a deist and rationalist to whom the mechanic laws of Nature were the providence of God; who was ineffably committed to conserve and reverence the sovereign freedom of the personal conscience: "Independence is my happiness, and I view things as they are, without regard to place or person; my country is the world, and my religion is to do good."

Emerson was a Unitarian and a Transcendentalist to whom Nature was the live flesh of an Oversoul that speaks in a unique fashion in each and every person and through each and every person: "We will walk on our own feet; we will

work with our own hands; we will speak our own minds";
we will be everywhere and always self-reliant, knowing that
each and every one of us brings the entire universe to a different focus in the integrities of our diverse singularities of self-
dependence.

Royce was an absolute idealist with Christian overtones.
The universe to him was an infinite, ineffable totality which
revealed itself as a "self-representative system" each element
of it unique yet entirely involved with the others and needing
to attain the fullest consciousness of the principles of its involvement. He disclosed the principle as "loyalty to loyalty,"
and by means of it was able to sanction the diversity of "regional and local loyalties." He sometimes described his philosophic faith as "absolute pragmatism."

Thoreau cannot be said to have formulated the philosophy
that he lived, except perhaps in his tract on the duty of civil
disobedience. His perspectives were all in his perception, his
perception of the natural scene at hand, not the symbolic one
of abstract conception and logical discourse. He practiced
the self-reliance and communion with Nature that Emerson
preached, and he had a feeling for the cosmic import of the
immediate that could be called a mystique of practicality: "In
any weather, at any hour of the day or night, I have been anxious to improve the nick of time, and notch it on my stick,
too; to stand on the meeting of two eternities, the past and the
future, which is precisely the present moment; to toe that
line."

Thoreau makes a not inept bridge to James and the later
Dewey—and their epigons—with their singularities of feelings
for the present as transition, their accent on futurity, process
and innovation as the metaphysical correlates of indefeasible
individuality and freedom. Emerson and Royce, and diver-
gently, Paine, had bespoken that recasting of the Newtonian
assured, of the Calvinist anxious, acquiescence in an inscruta-
ble foreordination into a voluntaristic individualism of freedom and hope, which is signalized as "the Genteel Tradition."
Freedom and hope are ultimately guaranteed by an infinite
omnipotent Being always and everywhere the same—a Being
eternal and universal which releases man's psyche from, and
compensates it for, the turbulent stream of strain and suffering,

the hardships of its changes and chances, that so mightily figure in the struggle to go on struggling which is also called the
will to live, the will to survive, and whose paramount problem
is "the problem of evil." James and Dewey envisioned no such
universe. Although James was preoccupied with plurality,
freedom, and the functioning will, while Dewey was concerned with unifications, orderings, and the functioning intelligence, both accepted for real what those others deprecated.
Thought, whether scientific or other, was to them a projection
and testing of a belief by working out its consequences, sym-
bolically or actually. Its validity or truth depended little or not
at all on what it was in itself. It might be a perception, an
image, a recollection, a concept denoted by a sign or a symbol.
It might be a constructed model or an actual thing or event.
It might be any of these alone or all together. Its truth or
validity could be the trust which a mind gave it as a prophecy
of the future; it could be the consequences composing the
future; or it could be the trust and consequences together.
Thinking comprehends a constant choosing between diverse
ways of reordering, remaking, transforming, confused and
hazardous situations. It comprehends the commingling of an
inner searching and seeking whose findings are creatings, and
an outward explanation whose findings are discoveries. Its intended consequences are such that whatever has obstructed or
contracted or perplexed and affrighted the thinker, *before* he
took thought, frees, facilitates and enhances his living *after* he
has taken thought.

Of course, his thought may fail of its intentions. But when
it succeeds, its operations may be rightly called sequent solutions of the problem of evil. This is their value, whether lasting
or unlasting; whatever they consist in: a clearing in a wilderness, a political clean-up in a city, a treatment and cure of a
disease in a medical center, a shift from scarcity to abundance
in an economy, an organization of battle and victory in a
competitive sport or a war, a shift from warfare to peaceful
competition in international affairs, a resolution of a mathe-
matical perplexity in a scholar's study, or solutions of problems
of physics, or chemistry or biology or psychology in corre-
sponding research laboratories. Whatever be the "problem-
atical" situation, it presents to the mind encountering it a

frontier with no path to follow, perhaps with none actually or imaginatively prevised. The mind must imagine and choose a path into the unknown and then cross the boundary, on its own responsibility, at its own risk. Its choice is an act of faith, a hazard of belief and more or less calculated risk, and the completeness of its commitment to its wager may make the deciding difference between winning and losing. For here commitment is faith and faith is courage and courage is reason in action. If, first, the will to live is the will to believe with all one's flesh and spirit, it becomes, last, the will to believe, not reflexly and blindly, but reflectively, with the light of the kind of knowledge which is power because it anticipates consequences. This faith illumined is the laborious fighting faith of the struggle for survival whereof the survival of the struggler consists. The struggle is a sequence of changes sustained by faith in a *What:* the struggler himself; in a *How:* his relations with other strugglers, their ways of living together, their instruments of recollection, communication, operation, and creation that combine into the collective economy of their culture. The collection becomes a configuration piecemeal. "It is not necessary," James wrote somewhere, "to attack the universal problems directly, and as such, in their abstract form. We work at their solution in every way—by living and by solving minor concrete questions, as they are involved in everything. The method of nature is patience and that easy-fitting faith, not tense but smiling, and with a dash of skepticism in it, which is not in despair at postponing a solution."

For an American, or anyone else whose faith is the American Idea, the *what* consists in the creed set forth as the Declaration of Independence, and the *how* in the code ordained by the amended and amendable social contract spelled out as the Constitution of the United States. Historically, the *what* and the *how* become the sequence of operations wherewith the American Idea as faith is incarnated in America as fact: the Civil War; the thrust across the continent which won the West; the transvaluation of the wastes and wilds of Nature into the natural resources of man; the creation of the sciences and the invention of the tools and the arts of their use wherewith natural resources are transubstantiated into national wealth. One American man of science signalizes all science as "the endless frontier." The human crux in this sequence is the believing will, the creative intelligence sustaining its powers and devising its plans on the gradient of the American Idea.

XIII. THE OVER-ALL AMERICANIZATION OF HUMAN RELATIONS

On this gradient also proceeds the changing of the frontiers between man and man which consummates the Americanization of human relations despite "cultural lag," "social Darwinism," né Calvinism, regional regressions and continental obstructions, diversions and subversions. "The truth is," William Graham Sumner of Yale had written, "that the social order is fixed by laws of nature precisely analogous to those of the physical order. The most a man can do [is] by his ignorance and conceit to mar the operation of the social laws." But believing Americans knew better, as de Tocqueville had noted some generations earlier. "The great privilege of the Americans," he had written, "does not consist in being more enlightened than other nations but in being free to repair the faults they commit." To Americans, Mr. Sumner's "social laws" were only conventions of that "certain blindness in human beings" which William James so graphically delineates and illuminates in his essay by that name. They kept on laboring to transvalue "social laws" into consequences of the American Idea; while the developments of modern physics has tended to confirm their faith by somewhat unfixing Mr. Sumner's "fixed laws of nature of the physical order." Their endeavors were piecemeal, disconnected, apparently tangent to one another. Yet all came, in the course of time, to a reciprocity of understanding and support.

We may count first "the woman's rights' movement," that arduous endeavor by the sex to eradicate the stigma of weakness, inferiority and deficiency laid upon women because they are women, aligning them with children and idiots. Women's struggle to Americanize the "androcentric culture" transplanted from Europe, into a human one realizing the American Idea, pervades all the branches of the national enterprise. The Suffrage movement was political; the Woman's Clubs formation was intellectual, esthetic, and civic. Signal was the extension of the housemother's feelings of responsibility to the housekeeping and health of the cities' schools and the cities' government. It is not simply that American women came to outnumber American men among the nation's teachers; it is that they became leading challengers of political misrule and economic peonage. By forming the Consumer's League, they each defined and applied the power of the buyer to modify the working conditions, the qualities of the material, and wages and workmanship of the workers who produced the goods they bought. It was a woman, Lillian Wald, and her associates, who initiated public health service by setting up the nurses' settlement in Henry Street, New York. It was a woman, Jane Addams, who, at Hull House in Chicago, brought the American Idea to bear upon the Americanization of the miserable, lost, anxious miscellany of ethno-cultural immigrant bands who did the back-breaking and soul-crushing dirty work on which the wealth and power of the cities live. It was this woman, too, who understood, savored and valued their cultural diversities, and liberated them at Hull House for expression and appreciation among their neighbors. Her initiatives led the way to changing the meaning of "Americanization" into greater consonance with the American Idea.

How women, gathering as women, in clubs and other groupings, have worked and fought their way to their present advanced position in the struggle for equal liberty is of record, and here needs no detailing. The case of working men as working men is similar. What is called "the labor movement" comprehends a slow, irregular, often violent and bloody, yet never surrendered struggle for equal liberty by Americans who work with their hands, on the land and on the sea, in mines, in shops, in factories and offices. Slowly they learned to pool their interests, unite their strengths, and confront their employers, where they could, with preponderant power; where they could not, with equal strength, in deciding the hours and wages of labor, the standards and conditions of work, the continuity of employment and the like. "Labor Movement" also comprehends the struggle within labor organization over the rights of workers differing in race, faith and sex to equality in union membership and employment over dishonest and exploitative leaderships, and over all the other alternatives to Americanization. Victories are signalized by the Clayton Act, which explicitly declares that human labor cannot be treated as an article of commerce, and by the general acceptance of the idea of "the dignity of labor," by trade-union educational and cultural enterprises, including bureaus of research and information to match those of managements; by the general displacement of the strike with arrangements for revising contracts by negotiation and arbitration. Most signal perhaps is the recognition that the doctrine which asserts that labor has no stake in the well-being and satisfaction of management (the usual, inaccurate word is "capital") is as false as its converse; now management also agrees that the prosperity of the industry is the security of the worker in it, and that concern for this prosperity is a legitimate responsibility of the trade-union.

Concurrent with this Americanization (so very much in contrast to a soi-disant "America Plan" of employer-employee relations in the national economy) has been the notable change in the attitude of "Capital" towards its own gains, well-gotten or ill-gotten. In any account of American industry the names Carnegie, Rockefeller, Frick, Guggenheim, Mellon, Ford have quite another aura and fragrance than such a name as Robert Owen or the Cadburys, or William Hapgood or even John Humphrey Noyes. They figure, in a good many connections, as "robber-barons" without ruth and without scruple, who amassed fortune and power, organized into "Big Business," by every means of force and fraud. Yet they, too, reshaped the figure of that image into harmony with the representative "American." "Big Business," wrote George Santayana, in *The Genteel Tradition at Bay*, "is an amiable monster, far kindlier and more innocent than anything Machiavelli could have anticipated, and no less lavish in its patronage of experiment, invention and finery than Bacon could have desired." Its avatars undertook, each in his own way, to contribute, from the profits of this "piracy," to the nurture of the democracy. They endowed, they even built, institutions of higher learning; they endowed or built museums of the fine arts; they set up pension plans for teachers; fellowships for promising young talent or matured abilities; they organized institutions of scientific research whose inquiries concern the bodily and spiritual health, not of Americans only, but of all the world's peoples. The agencies by which this is done are called "Foundations" and they operate with such wisdom as the conventions enable them to mobilize. One might call them the T.V.A.s of the free mind. They have become the Joneses of a "philanthropy" whom more and more Americans strive to emulate. Of course, the motives in play are neither simple nor single. But suffusing all of them, whatever they be, is a sort of perception that beyond comparatively narrow limits, a private fortune is a public trust, that the meaning of profits produced by Big Business is a public meaning, intrinsic to "the general welfare"; that in terms of the American Idea, to serve the general welfare is, on as nearly equal terms as the nature of things enables, "to secure these rights." So a Foundation such as the Rosenwald Foundation may elect for the vital center of its work, the cultural, and by consequence, the political equalization of Negro Americans; the Ford Foundation may endow agencies to develop adult education and to defend, secure, enhance civil liberties. Like the woman's movement and the labor movement, Foundations signalize projections of the American Idea into unAmericanized regions of the cultural economy. They figure among the differentiae of the Americanization of "capitalism" in the United States of America.

Something analogous was to be observed in the alterations of the intent and programs of "Americanization" themselves. They also were moved, not swiftly, and not without hardships, toward consistency with the American Idea.

XIV. CULTURAL PLURALISM IN THE FULFILLMENT OF THE AMERICAN IDEA

During the nation's early years, a newcomer's commitment to the Idea was sufficient. The public confession of this commitment, carried out according to law, was called "naturalization," and naturalization is still formally completed with the oath of allegiance casting off allegiance to all other governments and binding the swearer to that of the United States. But turns in events have diversified the formal requirements with informal ones, often little else than interventions of the propensities and prejudices of the sitting judges; in several instances, judicial denials of citizenship have been successfully appealed to the Supreme Court. Other questionings of naturalization had been postulated on the fraudulent practices of political machines which, in their rivalries, exploited the naturalization of aliens and aliens as citizens for their own advantage. Their operations had been in part offset by the efforts of social settlements to prepare their clients for the privileges and obligations of citizenship.

Especially and meaningfully "American" in the perspectives of the American Idea, had been the institution, all over the nation, of public evening schools which conducted classes for immigrants in the three R's and "citizenship." The nonpolitical, voluntary or philanthropic groups concerned to Americanize the immigrant increased in kinds and numbers. With the turn of the century, the progressive division of labor under machine industry multiplied and diversified the occupations of Americans. Desuetude in America had starved the skills which the peasant or craftsman immigrant had brought from abroad into the unskilled labor wherewith he earned his bread on these shores. Industrialization opened up to him semiskilled and then skilled occupations which required some degree of literacy. Great corporations producing automobiles, or other machinery, or chemicals, etc., etc., in due course found it profitable to set up classes which would the better conform their employees to their corporate requirements. These classes were often spoken of as engaged in Americanization. Soon or late, books of what I have called the Bible of America—recurrently, of course, the Declaration of Independence, the Constitution, Lincoln's Gettysburg Address—would figure in the reading matter: for children in the public schools, certainly, for grownups in the other schools and in the public evening schools probably.

Two generations of immigrants felt, as did natives, that Americanization could mean only such conformation to the "native," as would consume the newcomer's total cultural identity in identification with the "native": whatever native diversely meant across the continent. America would be a "melting-pot." Americanization would be "assimilation." The American man would be a blended man wherein all the later and lesser colors would be lost in the initial one. Nativist antipathy, nativist resistance to this sentiment led to a reappraisal by children and grandchildren of newer Americans of their transoceanic heritages. The form and purpose of their emulation changed. Original immigrant groupings, first gathered for self-help, fraternal communion, insurance, and other ends of common defense and support, added to their intention the record, the cultivation and preservation of their ethno-cultural pasts. Their emulation of the nativists now became communal as well as individual. They paralleled the Colonial Dames, the Daughters and the Sons of the American Revolution, in the Sons of Italy, the Ancient Order of Hibernians, the diverse Scottish, Welsh, German, Slavic, Jewish, Latin and other *landsmannschaften*. The purely personal communication with the relatives in the lands of their derivation, became collective and cultural ones. Pleasure visits acquired the quality of a religio-cultural pilgrimage, such as true believers make to Rome or Jerusalem or London. On the academic level organs of intercultural exchange were set up, such as the German-America Institute or the James Hazen Hyde Foundation. By and large, the immigrants' struggles for equality with the natives gave up identification as a means thereto. Instead, they cultivated the rejected difference and worked to secure acknowledgment that it was, in its own singularity of difference, as good as its betters and good for its betters. Americanization now came to denote the processes by which the diverse learn to know, to understand and to live with one another as good neighbors in equal liberty; Americanism came to denote the union of the diverse; the American, any person convinced of the American Idea, working and fighting in and through this union to bring it from faith to fact.

Thus, Americanization seeking a cultural monism was challenged and is slowly and unevenly being displaced by Americanization, supporting, cultivating a cultural pluralism, grounded on and consummated in the American Idea. The diversification of the economy with its manifold new occupations reënforced the process. Each industry generated a characteristic re-grouping of individuals already in union with many others in a multitude of ways. Each plant became a specific configuration of thoughts, tools, and things with its own specific science and art, couched in a characteristic terminology that becomes the stuff of a new tradition and that newer fellow workers take over from the older ones and pass

on to the still newer ones. Each occupation in due course gives
rise to characters, fables, symbols capable of imaginative projection as tale, poem or picture of the sort that keep recurring
in the periodical literature and every so often enter signally
into the wider stream of national expression. This process is
an orchestration of diverse utterances of diversities—regional,
local, religious, ethnic, esthetic, industrial, sporting and political—each developing freely and characteristically in its own
enclave, and somehow so intertwined with the others, as to
suggest, even to symbolize, the dynamic of the whole. Each
is a cultural reservoir whence flows its own singularity of expression to unite in the concrete intercultural total which is
the culture of America.

Note the word "intercultural." Its spread in usage is concurrent with the spread of two other words: "interfaith" and
"interracial." All three are comparative newcomers in common usage. All three denote conscious ends and conscious
means to attain the ends. All three are descriptive of the goals
and methods in a teamplay of churches and of governments,
urban, state and federal, as well as of voluntary *ad hoc* societies. The intent is in the common prefix: *inter*, which here
postulates the parity of the different and their free and friendly communication with one another as both co-operators and
competitors: it postulates that every individual, every society,
thus realizes its own being more freely and abundantly than
it can by segregation and isolation and struggle to go it alone.

These postulates are intrinsic to the American Idea. They
are why, regardless of intermittent segregative and isolationist
diversions, imperialist propulsions, or party politics, the over-
all foreign policy of the United States has been peaceful and
peace-seeking, addressed to international conciliation, arbitration, and co-operative association. It was American foreign
policy which broached the principle of nationalities as an international rule, the safeguarding of the equal rights of religious and cultural minorities as a condition of internal peace.
It was American statesmanship which fought the first World
War as a war to safeguard democracy from oppression, "to
make the world safe for democracy." The same statesmanship
proposed and effected the League of Nations as an international society which might maintain and insure peace.

Another kind of statesmanship achieved the Kellogg Pact, the sixty parties to which agreed not to resort to war as an instrument of policy. Later Administrations took the initiative in the Technical Aid Program (Point 4) and the Marshall Plan. Americans had a leading role in the formation of UNESCO of the United Nations Organization. The International Declaration of Human Rights, which the Assembly of the United Nations adopted, not quite a century and three quarters after the adoption of the Declaration of Independence, is a more detailed statement by representatives of all mankind, addressed to all mankind, of articles of the same faith that representatives of the American patriots addressed to all mankind on July 4, 1776.

The sequence listed above shapes up into a developing pattern. But with the Bill of Rights and the other Amendments to the Constitution, it is a sequence of battles fought and won in the interest of a lasting intersocial and interpersonal peace still remoter than words can tell. The individualism, the pluralism, the personal and social liberties, which are the stakes of the war of cultures whereof the battles are events, are articles of a faith striving, perhaps Sisyphus-like, to attain consummation in the present substance of the thing hoped-for, in the actual disclosure of the thing unseen. Like the meals we must needs eat daily in order to go on living, the battles of the faith in the American Idea must needs be fought and won daily if we are to go on living at peace with one another as free men. They must all the more imperatively be fought in these days when the totalitarian menace gathers unprecedented power and drive abroad, and the anxieties and fears it arouses at home nourishes a home-bred totalitarian enmity to the American Idea more subtle, more corrupting, more deadly because it does so in pretended loyalty.

The tension between an ancient authoritarian monism of culture and the free cultural pluralism intrinsic to the American Idea has been the vital spring of the nation's history. Throughout this history the American people's fighting faith in the Idea has kept it the preponderant force in their altering cultural economy. But now the balance shifts. The elements of the configuration change their relationships. Only the clear head and the clean heart, pledging anew its life, its fortune and its sacred honor to the Idea, committing them with all illusions stripped away, with the naked courage that knows and understands and will not yield, can sustain the preponderance and push forward, daily battle after battle, to the final peace which never is, but always is about to be.

If the third of the inalienable rights with which—so the Declaration of Independence affirms—God equally endows all men, carries any other than an ephemeral meaning, this is its meaning. What else, indeed, can "the pursuit of happiness" consist in? In view of the human condition, whether in a state of nature or the configurations of culture, can the pursuit be the transit from one evanescing excitement or pleasure to another, each no sooner experienced than forgotten? Must it not be the cultivation of an art of life, guided by faith and worked out by patterned conduct, the two together creating an individual biography or a communal history, the linkage of whose events is a practical orchestration of an imaginative vision of nature, man, and man's destiny? And if the pursuit of happiness be this, then the pursuit of happiness is the creation of cultures and the sporting union of their diversities as peers and equals; it is the endeavor after culture as each communion and each community, according to its own singularity of form and function, envisions its own cultural individuality and struggles to preserve, enrich, and perfect it by means of a free commerce in thoughts and things with all mankind. Cultural pluralism signalizes the harmonies of this commerce at home and abroad. It designates that orchestration of the cultures of mankind which alone can be worked and fought for with least injustice, and with least suppression or frustration of any culture, local, occupational, national or international, by any other.

II

COMMENTS AND DISCUSSION

THE SPIRIT OF CULTURAL PLURALISM

by Stanley H. Chapman

Lecturer in Sociology, University of Bridgeport
Lecturer in Sociology and Anthropology, Brooklyn College

Come, I will make the continent indissoluble
I will make the most splendid race the sun ever shone upon,
I will make divine magnetic lands
    With the love of comrades.[1]

Poets feel and by their feeling make poems of things, thoughts, and themes: the word prisms through which, if they and we are fortunately successful, we can share some of their feeling. Whitman was one of our more successful poets of America and Americans. It is to our glory and happiness that of much that has happened to us in our history it could be recorded, if we were now so wont,

Then was fulfilled that which was spoken by Whitman the prophet.

He was a poet to Kallen's taste—Kallen the American philosopher. Now philosophers are men who think and by their thinking make books or parts of books or sets of books, of things, thoughts, and themes. They must, to qualify as prophets, practice a kind of literary communicativeness, or possess an oracular omni-allusiveness, to enable their fellows and followers to say,

Then was fulfilled. . . .

Kallen's right so to be cited is based on the first of these philosophical attributes both by thought devoted to matters

[1] Walt Whitman, *Leaves of Grass*, New York, Random House, Modern Library Edition, 1921, p. 100.

of crucial moment, and by effective formulation. He himself reports that in his early formal training as a philosopher,

> . . . I realized that philosophy was not the impersonal vision of eternal being I had believed it to be. I came to see it as a man's endeavor after his personal salvation. . . .
>
> Philosophy, it came to me, is in actual life a method and instrument of adjustment, a human organ in the human struggle to survive. . . .[2]

This crucial contemporaneity makes possible an unusual contribution. Poster describes this philosophy at work.

> The foci of Kallen's thought and writing are so varied and yet so interdependent that it is impossible to isolate them. . . . They range from new forms of education in a democracy to a passionate and understanding concern about the fate of the Jewish people.[3]

A constant theme for him has been the relation of liberalism, freedom, and the individual. He has worked to the Whitman text:

> And nothing endures but personal qualities.[4]

In an autobiographical summary he has written:

> Although I feel philosophy as a calling and enjoy teaching it, I have not been able to devote myself exclusively to what is euphemistically known as "scholarship" and the sheer academic life. My earliest interests were as literary as philosophical and were soon crossed by direct participation in political and economic movements of the land, especially those aiming at the protection and growth of freedom, including the labor movement, the civil liberties union and the consumers' co-operative movement. Hence I have never attained that fullness of pedagogical withdrawal which custom and prejudice ordain for the practice of philosophy in America. Unable to separate my profession from my life, I have always found myself ill at ease with the philosophy

---

[2] Horace M. Kallen and Sidney Hook (eds.), "Philosophy Today and Tomorrow," *American Philosophy Today and Tomorrow*, New York: Lee Furman, Inc., 1935, p. 252.

[3] Sidney Ratner (ed.), "Liberalism and Horace M. Kallen," a review of *Vision and Action—Essays in Honor of Horace M. Kallen on his 70th Birthday, Congress Weekly*, N.Y., American Jewish Congress, June 28, 1954, 21: 23:14-15.

[4] *Op. cit.*, p. 161.

and the psychology of the schools. The first has seemed to me for the most part a ceremonial liturgy of professionals as artificial and detached from the realities of the daily life as bridge or chess or any other safe but exciting game of chance, and much of the second has seemed to me the sedulous elaboration of disregard for the living man of flesh and blood.[5]

His first section discusses the meaning of culture, he

whose constant preoccupation, philosophically and politically, was to extend the individual's sense of freedom and enjoyment of life within our economic and political order.[6]

Culture understood as the part of experience not devoted to vocation, as consumption after satisfying the demands of occupation—culture so understood subsumes the life that the individual can consider his own. Between it and the sociologists' and anthropologists' definition there is a chapter of American economic and political history. The second definition runs (and about it there is some possible cavil)—a culture is the sum of the material and nonmaterial adjustments of a society to its environments, the complete way of life of a group of people.

The distinction between culture as non-vocation and as a way of life has two significances. First, it suggests individual rejection of the occupational necessities, acceptance of whatever can be enjoyed of available experience off the job. Acceptance operates in terms of the things, thoughts, and themes available in the continental U.S.A. to all not on the job. Second, culture as non-vocation and as a way of life suggests that what group habits the American resident or citizen practices—on or off the job—are a part of the American culture, or way of life. Understood—the individual practices the regional or other variations of the national way of life prevailing wherever he may find himself: he does not practice the whole continental culture with its innumerable alternatives. No one does, or can.

The immigration history approach traditional to social science has assumed a quasi-ghetto or part old-country, old-region culture brought by groups to new American residence-

[5] *Op. cit.*, p. 250.
[6] Poster, *op. cit.*, p. 14.

work sites. In describing resultant phenomena—real states of affairs such as second-generation conflict, the immigrant-migrant ladder, *allrightnick*ism, passing, the A.P.A., the K.K.K., anti-Semitism, Coughlinism, fundamentalism, McCarthyism—in describing phenomena resulting from international and internal migration, the social scientist has perhaps oversimplified. He has occasionally studied only culture of departure, culture conflict of migration, and receiving or host culture.

Assimilation is the key supplementary concept.[7] Out of Chicago by insight, the term describes the behavior dynamics of the group newly come to an established society, who come, after a purgatory stage called *conflict* (characterizing the period of being unable to comprehend the new culture, as well as of being incapable of being comprehended and accepted as partners in any part of the host culture), to qualify as practitioners of the established ways in their essentials. The new group has undertaken a journey toward likeness with the previously established inhabitants. The next and final step, *amalgamation*, involves biological-social intermingling: the new group becomes sufficiently like the established group to intermarry and completely to join the established community.

A second possible step, *accommodation*, is here omitted. It is characterized by such behavior as will minimize conflict short of assimilation. It implies a ghetto base, allowing creature survival of the group removed, except for minimum necessary contact with the surrounding society. It is the goal, otherwise described, of the anti-assimilationist.

Kallen's prophetic tour de force has been to demand an enlargement of focus from the immigrant and migrant groups to the whole national scene. The standard of living has proliferated; some would say, improved. The civic estate has grown. This is not something that has arrived by and of itself. There have been men and the trends of which they were a part, such men and women working changes in our national way of life as Jane Addams, Thomas A. Edison, Edward A. Filene, Henry Ford, John L. Lewis, Jacob A. Riis, Franklin D. Roosevelt, Margaret Sanger, Charles P. Steinmetz, Eli Whitney.

[7] Robert E. Park and Ernest W. Burgess, *Introduction to the Science of Sociology.* Chicago: University of Chicago Press, 1921, Ch. VIII-XI, pp. 505-784.

Because of our proliferating national culture, the lot of the specific citizen today is different from that of a century, a generation, a decade ago. Industrialization has done much. Today there are perhaps more boring jobs than ever before in the world's economy, but fewer of them are deleterious to life and health. There are in our part of the world no galley slaves. We have fled so far from forced child labor that perhaps a factor in juvenile delinquency may be that legal age of employment arrives appreciably later than age of biological, intellectual, and social capacity.

We live in an off-the-job culture rich in creature comfort and insistently advertised. The yearning for new products before the old are used up, or in many cases paid for, promises or threatens to replace real or merely sentimental vestiges of ancestral cultures. The whole culture of origin was left upon migration. The question now is: are you a normal, happily dissatisfied, American consumer?—not: are you a loyal Guelph or Ghibelline?

Kallen the consumer adviser can not find the same satisfaction in our streamlined, nationally advertised economy as can Kallen the friend of labor, academic democracy, free men and women able to respect themselves in their work. When all have bread, there is perhaps a Gresham's law operating at the pastry table—but there are few rickets, little starvation. Colorful men's fashions—California's switch of women's hats to men's furnishings—may constitute a departure from established male decorum. Fashion frequently has been at variance with good taste. But the point is not one of breeding or aesthetics: seasonal fashion depends on designing for obsolescence; the society that discards last season's wardrobe can afford and does wear a new one. Furthermore, the faster seasonal fashion gyrates, the more standardized the mass produced tastes of the moment. The same production-distribution dynamics operate in all areas of our culture, encouraging new purchasers for old products, redesigning products, searching for new products—a process that affects dress, job, household, sports, and the myriad other types of consumption performed privately or socially. "It is the variety and range of his participations which does in fact distinguish a civilized man from an uncivilized," Kallen observes. "Such a man obviously orchestrates a growing pluralism of associations into the wholeness of his individuality."

" 'Cultural Pluralism' is a controversial expression." Only two groups (and Kallen, who knew what was happening) were even remotely interested, and they vitally. In point of urgency there were first members, spokesmen, or manipulators of "foreign" groups, who insisted with varying specificity and stridency that one could prefer tea in a glass, marriage by arrangement, Friday Sabbaths, Guelph as the language of intimacy, and still be entitled to all the rights, privileges, and perquisites of citizenship and American fellowship.

The advocates of cultural pluralism were such spokesmen of minorities as another immigrant philosopher has described: "Minorities are groups who expect and demand privileges the majority do not enjoy." Such proclaimers of cultural equality in our national orchestra of cultures were or (in the case of the Marxians) pretended to be enamored of the specific old-country culture aspects not practical or comfortable in the new country. They were by and large anti-assimilationist in practice if not intent. Prevailingly they appealed to nostalgia rather than to possibility. The foundering fallacy—in theory as in practice—of the minority culture integrity champions was an offense against Linton's categories of participation in culture.[8] These are *universals*, practiced by every appropriate member of the society, *alternatives* available to all, *specialties* peculiar to a recognized few, and *individual peculiarities* tolerated in some individuals. The fallacy of such champions lay in expecting to practice specialties without paying the cultural price of peculiarity. They dealt in cultural incommensurables.

The second group concerned with cultural pluralism have been students of the developing American population and culture. They have been scientifically, or by reason of place within the established culture, objective: they did not feel the emotional commitment of new people to old ways in a strange society. They observed groups in the migration-conflict-assimilation continuum; they did not feel like people off the boat or moving van.

Many professional minority members and social scientists

[8] Ralph Linton, *The Study of Man*. New York: D. Appleton-Century Company, 1936, Ch. XVI, pp. 271-287.

missed the point of what was happening. The first feared or feigned to fear deculturalization; the second thought of acculturation as a simple algebraic equation. One worked to preserve the in-group of the minority in its ways; the other, a professional In-group, observed minorities as out-groups endowed with varying capacities to approach the large In-group of the established community.

What Kallen has all along sensed, and so many others of us refused to see and to feel, is that our country is a true melting-pot. None of us immune, we are in fact producing a new people and a new way of life. Assimilation is a multiple process, in which there are strictly speaking no assimilators or assimilatees, in which there are merely participants in assimilation. The individual's "equipment constitutes his cultural mobility. . . . A living culture is a changing culture."

Elsewhere Kallen has spelled out the mechanics:

When a community, whatever be its size, decides some issue, it divides into a majority and one or more minorities. Our habits of thought and speech lead us to imagine such division as permanent. In free societies, however, it involves nothing static or fixed. An individual who is a member of a majority in one respect becomes a member of a minority in another, and vice versa. Each occupational group, each religious denomination, each political party, each sex, each race, set over against all the others, counts as a minority; associated with the others, as of the majority. Majorities are minorities in combination; minorities are majorities in division.

. . . Majorities are orchestrations of the different; minorities are dissociations of the different. The "American way" is the order of these constant combinations and dissociations in all the enterprises of living.[9]

In his present essay, Kallen again makes it plain that in our national life there is no majority, culturally speaking, pitted against minorities. He properly dispels that pathetic fallacy: in any specific cultural matter there may be one or more minorities distinct from, or opposed to, a temporary grouping of

[9] Horace M. Kallen, "National Solidarity and the Jewish Minority," *The Annals of the American Academy of Political and Social Science*, September 1942, Vol. 223, p. 17.

other minorities which for the time being act as a numerical majority.

One hypothetical exception might be taken to his treatment of minorities in American society. There is no disagreement over the first step: every person in America is a member of at least one ethnic minority; nor over the second: American ethnic minorities based upon language, country of origin, and religion are decreasingly cause for individual aloofness from the surrounding culture. A third, however, raises possibilities not dealt with here by Dr. Kallen. It is the hypothesis of the Four-fold Ethnoid Group Pattern,[10] according to which four families of American minorities appear to be assuming increasing importance, as the minorities themselves lose importance. For want of better terms, they may be called the Protestant, Catholic, Jewish, and Negro Ethnoid Groups. The four are carriers of discernible, more or less standardized variations on the prevailing national culture; the culture characteristics are not themselves ethnically derived as a patterned subculture, but the resulting subcultures appear to be ethnically transmitted—hence ethnoid.

The Protestant Ethnoid Group comprises those minorities practicing the American subculture whose core is derived from British Isles and Western European migration, who happen to have been or become Protestant (including the majority of the non-Roman Catholic and Orthodox denominations); the Catholic Ethnoid Group, minorities practicing Roman Catholicism and increasingly dominated by Irish Americans; the Jewish Ethnoid Group, minorities who have practiced or are practicing Judaism; the Negro Ethnoid Group, minorities who are anthropometrically Negro as well as those not considered

[10] The pattern emerged from undergraduate and graduate study under Prof. Maurice R. Davie. Certain reading was particularly helpful. James Bryce, *The Great Commonwealth*, New York: Macmillan, 1915, rev. 2 vols. Alexis de Tocqueville, *Democracy In America*, New York: P. F. Collier and Son, copyright 1900, translated by Henry Reeve, 2 vols. Andre Siegfried, *America Comes of Age*, translated by H. H. Hemming and Doris Hemming, New York: Harcourt, Brace and Co., 1927. Charles A. and Mary R. Beard, *The Rise of American Civilization*, New York. Macmillan, rev. ed., 1935. Elin L. Anderson, *We Americans*, Cambridge: Harvard University Press, 1937. Ruby Jo Reeves Kennedy, "Single or Triple Melting Pot?" *American Journal of Sociology*, January 1944, Vol. 49, p. 4, pp. 331-339. The necessity of a fourth group was suggested by Prof. Alfred McClung Lee.

white, who find their non-white position in our society in terms of the locally prevailing Negro subculture. These groups are admittedly not commensurate. If the pattern has any utility, it is descriptive of what is happening on the American minority front.

The four groups appear to define acceptable intermarriage, easy religious transfer, natural social intercourse, and to a limited degree education. The first group has left its mark on national institutions. The prestige of the four has been in order of recitation, although the details of the pattern are in constant adjustment and vary with both time and place.

Cultural pluralism as orchestration of diversity—such is Kallen's theme. It is the pluralism of philosophy—recognition of multiple ultimates. Orchestration of diversity emphasizes the *together* quality. The dichotomy of self-obliterating conformity or ghetto shows itself false. "The diversification of the economy with its manifold new occupations reinforced the process," Kallen reminds us, of displacing the chimera of Americanization by cultural monism with the reality of Americanism by consonant diversity. Each occupation has its subsociety and subculture, contributing to the over-all American culture, unifying and diversifying it—as do the "regional, local, religious, ethnic, esthetic, industrial, sporting, and political" enclaves. "Each is a cultural reservoir whence flows its own singularity of expression to unite in the concrete intercultural total which is the culture of America." Intercultural, interfaith, interracial—these are the practices which portend increasing fulfillment of the American Idea.

Here we have an American philosophy. Nowhere, perhaps, is our national development so cogently portrayed: the heart of the matter is people; then how they earn their livings, what they consider to embody living worth the earning, what they do to each other in pursuit of earning and living together, where they are going: what their children and their children's children will be like.

We students of the American scene, as well as participants in it, are fortunate in having so perceptive and eloquent a companion, teacher, and fellow citizen as Dr. Kallen. He has studied, worked, written. He has made of his career and philosophy a prophecy—instructive, corrective, inspiring.

His two closing sentences give to this analytical essay a continuing prophetic promise. It is the same promise from analysis that Lord Acton spoke in 1895:

> . . . where there has been long and arduous experience, a rampart of tried conviction and accumulated knowledge, where there is a fair level of general morality, education, courage, and self-restraint, there, if there only, a society may be found that exhibits the condition of life towards which, by elimination of failures, the world has been moving through the allotted space. You will know it by outward signs: Representation, the extinction of slavery, the reign of opinion, and the like; better still, by less apparent evidences: the security of the weaker groups and the liberty of conscience, which, effectually secured, secures the rest.[11]

It is the same promise Whitman sang in 1855:

And thou America,
Thy offspring towering e'er so high, yet higher Thee above all
    towering,
With Victory on thy left, and at thy right hand Law;
Thou Union holding all, fusing, absorbing, tolerating all,
Thee, ever thee, I sing.[12]

[11] John E. E. D. Acton, "Inaugural Lecture on the Study of History," Ch. I in *Essays on Freedom and Power*, selected by Gertrude Himmelfarb, New York: Meridian Books, p. 37.
[12] *Op. cit.*, p. 175.

A REACTION TO KALLEN'S ESSAY

by Stewart G. Cole

Formerly Educational Director, South Pacific Division, National Conference of Christians and Jews

The study of cultural pluralism has intrigued Horace M. Kallen for a long time. Forty years ago he presented a series of articles in *The Nation* in which he discussed the problem of acculturation of the peoples flooding into this country from Europe. Then his concern was to combat the notion of the melting-pot. It represented a popular viewpoint among many social liberals. From Kallen's point of view it vitiated democratic practice in multi-culture America. He insisted upon the recognition of the integrity of transmitted cultures from the old world, the right of ethnic peoples to be different, and the obligation of the government of the United States to respect and protect multiple-group ways of living.

The current essay, "Cultural Pluralism and the American Idea," carries this issue a major step further. Earlier Kallen addressed himself to the problem of safeguarding freedom and insuring differences. Now he is accenting the need for accepting social responsibility and achieving a high quality of national unity. He examines the concepts of cultural pluralism *and* the American Idea to point out wherein each concern is short-changed without the enlistment of the other, and to support a fusion of these ideas. Only thus can the process of "Americanization" accomplish its proper purpose.

The influences of William James and Henri Bergson are clearly traceable in the essay; the author draws upon a rich literary and philosophical lore to support his thesis. He hammers home his convictions repeatedly by capitalizing upon illustrative situations out of the societies of ancient Rome,

Greece and Palestine, as well as from the development of Western civilization.

Kallen's critique of the social history of this country turns over much fallow soil. He traces the devastating effects upon the individual and society alike of the tendency of our people to bifurcate their life into work and leisure-time activities. He lays bare the iniquities of social, political, economic and religious authoritarianism. They include In-group chauvinism and Out-group stereotypy, intergroup rivalry and conflict, interpersonal prejudice, interracial segregation, and pressure and counter-pressure between In- and Out-groups to acquire a larger share of the materiel of the good life. The essayist illustrates the repeated subversion of the American Idea as, for instance, in the current practice of social hysteria and patriotic orthodoxy. Kallen is quick to sense that, time and again, the resurgence of real democracy has redeemed this country. As often as not it emerged out of unofficial or obscure places, but was nonetheless effective.

Quoting Znaniecki and Northrop, the author believes that "culturalism rather than nationalism . . . is the rising fact of the world today," and that the road to peace lies in the direction of building a "world culture." Unity here, if stable *and* dynamic, will rest upon the principles of political and economic pluralism, "a union on equal terms of sovereign and independent diversities." Human independence and interdependence must remain the bi-polar forces of the social axis in such a "one-world" movement.

This essay is a clear testimony to a philosophy of American citizenship by one of its most astute, courageous, and longtime exponents. Its freshness of approach lies in the adoption of a socio-cultural frame of thinking through which the author traces the ups and downs of American devotion to the ideals of democracy.

Is Kallen equally judicious in his treatment of the part that religion has played in shaping our way of life? I doubt it. The conviction that the religious groups do suffer from cultural lag which impedes the hazardous, strenuous tempo of the democratic movement, is one I share. Anthropomorphic and mythological beliefs do weight down the lives of many religious people, though these beliefs are not always their primary motivations in everyday social living. The Judaeo-Christian tradition has repeatedly had an elevating effect upon Western civilization. It has abetted the causes of social freedom and ethical responsibility on many fronts and on significant historic occasions. True, multiple sects and faiths do confuse our communal interests through their competitive appeals to absolute systems of loyalty. However, these same religious people have often marshalled humanitarian attitudes, improved standards of living, and rededicated themselves to the good, the true and the beautiful, which dignify human life and strengthen the cause of the American Idea.

COMMITMENT, BIAS, AND TOLERANCE

by Elizabeth F. Flower

Associate Professor of Philosophy, University of Pennsylvania

---

The essay that begins this book is a gem-like statement of Kallen's social philosophy of cultural pluralism which has been in the making for more than four decades. It bears witness dramatically to the intimate relation between culture and work which he there establishes and it portrays the faith of a great American in a noble idea. It would be most presumptuous of me here to review the qualifications of Kallen as a spokesman for democratic ideals, for they are common property. He speaks to the integrity of the individual and his actions have contributed in large measure to secure freedom and tolerance whether it be in civil, social, intellectual or aesthetic matters. Everywhere he has defended the right of the minority to be heard and the need of the majority to be educated. Here is a man who is not only content to talk about a way of life but who takes a hand in its forging.

All too frequently men of thought have been satisfied to remain aloof. Many well remember Felix Cohen's impassioned words before a meeting of professional philosophers which had concerned itself with the clarification of ethical terms and the verifiability of statements in the social sciences. He said (I give the gist but not the eloquence) that he had come to a meeting on ethics and social philosophy not to hear sterile debates on semantic and scientific issues but to learn what rights justice alone guarantees to individuals who have no privileged status conferred by place of birth or citizenship. Kallen expresses something of this same concern for action and the poverty of philosophic analyzing in his *Selbstdarstellung:*

My earliest interests were as literary as philosophical and were soon crossed by direct participation in political and economic movements including the labor movement, the Civil Liberties Union and the consumers' co-operative movement. Hence I have never attained that fullness of pedagogical withdrawal which custom and prejudice ordain for the practice of philosophy in America. Unable to separate my profession from my life, I have always found myself ill at ease with the philosophy and the psychology of the schools. The first has seemed to me for the most part a ceremonial liturgy of professionals as artificial and detached from the realities of the daily life as bridge or chess or any other safe but exciting game of chance, and much of the second has seemed to me the sedulous elaboration of disregard for the living man of flesh and blood.[1]

Now no one who has the least social conscience or sensitivity to the magnitude of the problems of social maladjustment, political ineptness and nuclear power has not felt the attraction of "overt action," of "doing something." Sometimes it requires self-discipline and even courage to remain in an ivory tower, examining and clarifying the conditions upon which action must be based if it is to be rational (and Kallen is surely in agreement). The role of vision, of poetry and persuasion is not the role of analyzing and criticizing; where the projects of the former are incompatible and inconsistent with the blueprints of the latter they are not substantial. Now I have neither the capacity nor the desire to challenge so enriching and inspiring an idea as that presented by Kallen. I do take it to be my task to raise some of those "tiresome," "liturgical" and "detached from reality" questions which are part of the heritage of the essay and upon which vision must rest if it is not to be taken as blind commitment. To do this I must forego a discussion of much in the chapters that commands the acquiescence of most and the respect of all thoughtful people and turn to issues which are clearly outside the essay and its intention; they are questions and comments that might be more appropriately addressed to the "scientific" in "scientific humanism" as Kallen's thought has been characterized. What follows, then, has no quality of disagreement but only of a request for elaboration and clarification; it stems from a concern to em-

---

[1] Sidney Hook and Milton R. Konvitz (eds.), *Freedom and Experience.* Essays presented to Horace M. Kallen, N.Y., Cornell University Press, 1947, Preface, p. viii.

phasize the indispensability of a critical point of view (to which Kallen, of course, is not inimical) and to elicit in the reprise responses of interest both to Kallen and his readers.

Among the more serious problems that face a scientist when he seeks to increase the certainty and scope of his knowledge is the need to examine and make explicit the assumptions which underlie it and the principles by which he systematizes and organizes it—in short a critique of his method.[2] The task of scrutinizing the method may be less exciting than the inquiry itself, but both indicate that scientific conclusions must not be regarded as anything but tentative, corrigible and recallable in the light of future experience.

Within the field of ethics, law and the social sciences the situation requires even greater caution, for those dealing with the normative not only inherit the problems common to all empirical sciences such as the nature of induction, ordering, probability, etc., but add their own particular difficulties about the status of value statements, especially when it is claimed that they are true, valid or justified. I expect to raise issues of this latter kind with respect to "Cultural Pluralism" and issues of clarity characteristic of scientific enterprise generally with respect to "of Meanings of Culture" and "Culture and the American Idea."

Of course problems of clarity, meaning, confirmation, verification and the distinction (if any) between statements of truth and value are all interrelated, and the manner of their relating makes for the positions and isms in contemporary philosophy. For example, operationism takes the meaning of a concept to be given by a set of procedures. I am not asking Kallen to solve these problems, but rather to consider their relevance for they seem particularly important when asking what may legitimately be predicated of culture and American culture. Neither am I riding any position of my own here save one that takes these issues seriously, for unconsidered philosophic loyalties are as out of place as any other unexamined loyalty. But we must be sure first that we are talking sense—that the terms we are using and their combinations into propositions and theories are reasonably precise and unambiguous. And secondly

2 Laurence Foster (ed.), "Examination of Some Assumptions in the Social Sciences," by E. Flower, *An Introduction to the Social Sciences.*

that we do not take even the most cherished of our ideals to be certain and beyond the need for clarification and modification. To do so is to pass emotionally charged slogans for ideas. Thus, for example, if anyone had stopped to examine "the supremacy of the Aryan race" (or of the White, for that matter) it would have become immediately apparent that either the phrase was nonsense or that it was tautological, unsupportable or false according to the meaning assigned. Likewise Hegel's dialectic and some interpretations of Marx are patently unserviceable as scientific theses of history. They may provide interpretations of events already past, but then any mathematician can provide a formula for, say, the length and interval of the reigns of the Georges; the problem is to find an interpretation or a formula that will predict the next moment of history. This the dialectic does not do not so much because it predicts incorrectly, but more insidiously, because it has placed itself beyond the reach of any disconfirming evidence whatsoever.

Let us restate some of the issues of the essay before considering the appropriateness of considerations above, which are not so grave for the matter at hand as may have been suggested since what I want to force is precisely the difference between Kallen's concepts and question-begging ones. Kallen's examination of culture takes on breadth and scope as the essay approaches its climax; the antiphony of culture and vocation develops in his conclusion into an integrated and complex harmony. The complete dichotomy of consummatory night and productive day, succeeded by the recognition of vocation as a necessary evil and of culture as a consequence of labor, finally becomes a reciprocal relation between the two. This lays the foundation on a cultural level for the point Commager makes on a political one: that the historical achievement and ideology of American democracy has depended upon the capacity and opportunity for free association and for equally free withdrawal.

The theme is utilized in a context which Kallen made famous in *Assimilation and Democracy*. He opposes the ideal of a melting pot, of the molding of a single Americanism from diverse cultural patterns, with his idea of cultural pluralism which is proposed here both as a fact of social interaction and as an American ideal of the relation of ethnic groups. As a fact, Kallen says diversity will always characterize culture whether it evolves naturally from within the group or is imposed from without; as an ideal, he associates "a nation of nations" with the democratic idea which holds that difference must not be equated with inferiority. The pluralism of which he writes is not absolute but relative; its individuals are neither to be isolated nor forced into a unity but by interacting and communicating with one another "struggle to provide and maintain the common means which nourish, assure, enhance, the different and often competing values they differently cherish."

The second chapter considers philosophical issues, the third relates cultural pluralism to the ideology and history of the United States. The American Idea is a cultural ideal which is based on the individual and his responsibility, while remaining faithful to his own community, to respect and associate with others. The struggle to transact it (the American Idea) from an article of faith into the eventuations of history is the vital center of American culture.

As was indicated above, my concern about the first and third chapters really constitutes a plea for elaboration, especially with respects to the word "culture" both singly and when coupled with "American." Kallen has already indicated the ambiguity of the word, its misuse as "Kultur" as well as its liberating and all-embracing character; what I should like to know further is what are the restrictions on the permissible predicates of culture. Is he thinking in terms of a system of universal predicates for cross cultural reference, and if so are they empirical or abstract (e.g. *Machtmensch* or *Kunstmensch*)? This does not come to a debate about the meaning of "culture," for definition of such a term must depend on what is fruitful for understanding and explaining data.

Similar problems arise with "American." Sometimes it intends a description, and that offers the obvious (though not insurmountable) difficulty to whom and how many must a characteristic pertain if it is to be properly used. This isn't as foolish as it sounds for how does one decide that Americans are not malicious or are pragmatic, or do respect the dignity and worth of the individual (despite the behavior of motorists, of racial and religious prejudice, etc.). An English reviewer of Commager's *The American Mind* says, "in America the digest and book club flourish. In fact for any interpretation of the character of the contemporary American and of the American way of life, all considerations of American creative intellect could be ignored, and in its place the observer might well watch the crowds at the Rose Bowl or the World Series, the families grouped around their television sets, the undergraduates at fraternity initiations, the housewives at women's club meetings and their husbands at Rotary, Elks or Kiwanis." [3] It is perhaps easy to reject this portrait, but what are the principles by which a more accurate one can be drawn.

Frequently "American" refers to a description not of our overt behavior but of how we want to act or believe we ought to act. Kallen often uses the word in this sense and intends, I suspect, a rather Jamesian or self-fulfilling prophecy. Thus he says, "Thus, Americanization seeking a cultural monism was challenged and is being slowly and unevenly displaced by Americanization, supporting, cultivating a cultural pluralism, grounded on and consummated in the American Idea." And more clearly in discussing "intercultural," "The intent is in the common prefix: *inter*, which here postulates the parity of the different and their free and friendly communication with one another as competitors as well as co-operators; it postulates that every individual, every society, thus realizes its own being more freely and abundantly than it can by segregation and isolation and struggle to go it alone."

When the essay proposes (rather than describes) goals to be achieved and recommends some ideals rather than others, then it must face the general problems of justification and validation and their relation to commitment. How does one decide between competing and incompatible goals and what are the criteria for such judgments? I suspect that Kallen's thinking here is along the pragmatic lines indicated by his discussion of James and Dewey; but it would be profitable to have his own view of this vexing problem spelled out since they must have been formed under fire. Roscoe Pound, speaking of himself, said, ". . . it is the habit of those who presume to speak with the voice of America to talk about the American way of life

[3] *Times* Literary Supplement, November 17, 1950.

. . . the American way of life always turns out to be the speaker's own way of life . . . the speaker's own dream. . . . For there are innumerable American ways of life, innumerable American Dreams."[4] But of course we do value some dreams above others, take some to be better or nobler than others, and I am concerned here with the grounds that make such decisions more than allegiance. Even if it were within my province, this would scarcely be the place to review the debates which "cultural pluralism" occasioned. This has been done often enough elsewhere. As recently as 1954 Nathan Glazer,[5] writing about the effects of a "third generation response," a kind of romanticized affinity for the country of origin, begins with an account of its influence. Rather I shall raise three problems concerning intergroup relations that call for elaboration of the second chapter. Kallen has certainly discussed these issues, but to my knowledge he has not handled them directly; as their clarification is critical to his theme and necessary to its understanding they are appropriate here.

In a less heroic mood than Kallen's the first point concerns exactly what elements or phases are referred to by "culture" in "cultural pluralism." As a definition of a subject matter it may be satisfactory to regard culture as the total complex of the "secondary environment which man creates in altering his surroundings" and to include thereby the consideration of all artifacts and systems of customs from political institutions to language, ideas, habits and techniques. However, to speak significantly of the relation that one culture has to another, it is imperative to be explicit about the factors being related. This was what was intended above when a definition of culture was invited. As was also indicated above, there surely is no single definition of "culture"; but if the term is to serve in an explanatory rather than emotive context it must be reasonably specific. Anthropologists have learned to be cautious about using such terms as "marriage" as if it referred to one phenomenon among Mohammedans, Catholics and Buddhists; infinitely greater pains are required when dealing with cultures that

[4] Laurence Foster (ed.), *An Introduction to the Social Sciences*, Ch. 4: "The American Heritage," by Roscoe Pound.
[5] Nathan Glazer, "Ethnic Groups in America: From National Culture to Ideology," *Freedom and Control in Modern Society*, Van Nostrand, 1954, p. 158.

they be commensurate. Empirical terms are never beyond revision and correction, but they cannot shift in mid-discussion
and their power is always a function of their clarity. The literature of comparative ethics illustrates the matter. The conclusions of those who determine the morality of an individual
or a group by an appeal to overt actions will seem to contra-
dict conclusions derived from a study of what is thought (or
said) to be right or good. But of course there is no contradiction where the issue is not joined.

It has seemed to me that Kallen has generally been concerned with the latter, with the interplay in the United States
of aspirations, preferences, goals and obligations that derive
wholly or in part from religion, race and original nationality.
For want of a better expression, let us call these "value-orderings" or "value-sets." Now, if what Kallen means by "cultural
pluralism" is that no set of values is to be condemned out of
hand because it is different, the belief of a minority (or majority, for that matter), or characteristic of persons having
certain physical traits, then he is spokesman for most, possibly
all, thoughtful persons. But I very much doubt that Kallen
would concert the recognition that diversity and difference are
not *per se* grounds of inferiority into an uncritical acceptance
of diversity for its own sake. Perhaps few problems arise when
communities having dissonant value-sets live in a sort of dis-
junctive symbiosis, but intercourse and exchange create major
problems of assessment and sacrifice. Orchestration is neither
inevitable nor easy; it cannot be achieved by allowing each
section to play their own themes in whatever tempo and key
are convenient. Thus the second point requiring discussion is
the manner of resolving competing and conflicting values.
Alain Locke puts it: "For the complete implementation of the
pluralistic philosophy it is not sufficient merely to disestablish
authoritarianism and its absolutes; a more positive and constructive development of pluralism can and should establish
some effective mediating principle for situations of basic value
divergence and conflict."[6] The third point extends the issue
and would inquire of Kallen what considerations beyond an
unqualified respect for another's values are relevant to the
forging of mutually constructive enterprises.

[6] Sidney Hook and Milton R. Konvitz (eds.), *op. cit.* p. 63.

These situations of basic value divergence and conflict constitute some of our gravest and most insistent difficulties. For
example, how does relativistic pluralism speak to the paradox
of toleration; must one group, which rates highly a respect for
others and co-operation, extend that tolerance to another
group whose primary objectives include the domination or displacement of the former. Point-Four programs and UNESCO
and their domestic counterparts present similar problems. No
doubt everyone prizes health, for example, or economic security, but their purchase price varies, that is to say, although
they will appear on most orderings of preferences or obligations but in different places. The imposition of hygiene and
efficient modes of production have often enough involved dis-
ruption of the original value-orderings; few wish to leave im-
poverished or underdeveloped peoples to their own devices,
but most are uneasy about disturbing integrated patterns even
when those patterns are indifferent to "progress."

Mexicans such as Dr. Mario Aquiler, director of the
UNESCO Pilot Project in Nayarit, and Dr. Manuel Gamio,
head of Interamerican Indian Affairs, have been working
concretely with situations created by social, racial, economic and religious diversity. Doubtless the "Europeanized"
have to be educated to a concern and an unsentimental respect
for Indian ways; but the principal task is to educate the Indian
to social and political responsibility. Gamio came ultimately
to regard Pre-Colombian archaeology as a means of awakening self-respect and a feeling of continuity with the past. Cultural missions and Indian schools seek to reënforce those aesthetic, social and moral traits that will lead to the incorporation
of the Indian in the national life and to a role in "*forjando una
patria*" which has a stronger ring than "forging a country."
But such a program requires the correction and even the ex-
tirpation of other traits, of beliefs intimately connected with
their *Weltanschauungen*, of economic aspirations, even of
basic personal relations.

Accommodation is inevitable. Perhaps the best laid plans
will little affect social processes, but we are not thereby ex-
cused the responsibility of attempting to make those adjustments as rationally and inexpensively as possible. Toleration
and willingness to appreciate values other than our own is as

important a condition for comprehensive social planning as an open mind is for scientific investigation. It is not sufficient to pursue non-interfering ends but to develop co-operative ones (which is, of course, different from uniform ones). The formulation of these goals offers serious problems which have just begun to be studied. We must investigate criteria for distinguishing genuinely incompatible value-sets from those which only appear to be so (an issue of importance in this polarized world) and also the nature and variety of co-operative relationships one set may have to another.

Scientific, including social, explanations are not ordinarily taken to be certain nor even unique; they are hypotheses that are always open to modification and recall. We may not be allowed the luxury of suspended judgment when social action is required, but there is even more reason to hold our commitments open to re-examination and review. This may be the most difficult kind of toleration to achieve.

REFLECTIONS OF A WAYFARING
LAYMAN

by Frank P. Graham

Representative for India and Pakistan, United Nations

At the outset of these comments I wish to say that I am not a sociologist, a social psychologist, an anthropologist or a culturologist. I am, accordingly, not competent to write a professional review or critical appreciation of Professor H. M. Kallen's treatise on "Cultural Pluralism." However, I am moved, in response to the request of the editor, and in appreciation of Professor Kallen's brilliant and evocative analysis and interpretation, to write these comments as a wayfaring layman. I shall not attempt to appraise the full import of his three chapters, I. The Meaning of Culture; II. Concerning the Varieties of Culture; and III. Culture and the American Idea.

As footnotes to his essay as a whole, I am giving some impressions of what to me are his most timely interpretations. I shall make some representative quotations which carry the development and significance of his main considerations and make some observations of my own which are corollary to or were evoked by his thinking and emphasis.

His thinking is timely for the people of the United States as they stand confronted with and are deeply involved in the impact on American culture of: (I) modern industrialism with its mass regimentations of American workers; and (II) the challenge of totalitarianism with its threats and pressures of tyranny and aggression from without and for conformity and uniformity from within. His analysis of the cultural incidence of industrial assembly lines and of totalitarian pressures makes most timely his emphasis on the need for the reassertion of the values of cultural pluralism as a basic part of the originally

revolutionary, the historically evolutionary, the humanely
hopeful and the democratically creative American Idea.

I. THE CULTURAL IMPACT OF INDUSTRIAL ASSEMBLY LINES ON
INDUSTRIAL WORKERS

In discussing the cultural impact of assembly lines on industrial workers Professor Kallen makes vivid the fact that mass
production makes for a regimentation of the workers which
is "imposed by the configuration of the plant and the character
of the equipment. The place of the worker is not chosen as an
act of free enterprise among companies of his own choice at
his own risk." Rather, "his place is predetermined by his specific assignment in a division of labor already prescribed by
the structure of the automatic machine at which he operates,
or the conveyor system which determines what operation he
shall repeat, how, and when, and how often he shall repeat it,
during eight hours of his working day." Furthermore, "the
sequential pattern made by the moving parts of a stationary
machine, or the ordered tempo of a conveyor system, is imposed, not chosen. No operative is himself a craftsman making
a whole shoe, a whole shirt, a whole automobile or a whole
anything. He is only a fraction of such a craftsman—1/500
more or less—of a craftsman. The complete factory is the
craftsman."

Moreover, "as for the product, the operations have no personal import. It does not matter who performs them. The operators serve as impersonally as any replaceable machine part."

In general, "our industrial economy," he goes further to
point out, "makes producer, distributor, consumer interdependent, but the interdependence is blind and unaware,
imposed from without, not perceived, understood, and consciously realized from within. Minus such insight and realization, the interdependence of the factory operatives is like that
of the parts of a clock or any other interlocking mechanism;
their role is as gadgets of a machine, not members of the community."

He emphasizes that it is by this impersonal regimentation of
workers who earn their wages by mechanically automatic
work, that the separation is made deeper between "vocation"
and "culture." It is, he says, in "the commonsense of those

gainfully employed individuals" that "it is the spending of what they earn, not the earning of what they spend, that is postulated as the experience of culture. Their common sense opposes culture to vocation. The prejudices or principles of the 'cultured classes' exalt and consecrate this antithesis, and enshrine it in the conception of the 'liberal education,' traditionally interpreted as the education befitting a free man, which shapes into a being of 'culture and refinement.' Their commonsense assimilates vocation to labor and culture to leisure. . . . Their labor is a servile necessity and their leisure is a condition of freedom, both as active and passive. These sequences [of daytime work and evening or nighttime leisure] signalize culture as the ultimate consumer of what vocation produces. . . . It is enough to establish the observation that we earn by day, working, and spend by night, living; that we live by our vocations and live in our cultures; that the traditional distinction between vocation and culture is not essential but contingent."

Professor Kallen, in thus pointing up the deep divorce of vocation, with its mechanical and automatic nature, from culture, is traditionally conceived, reminds us that "the segregation of culture and vocation" has both a Greek and an Hebraic-Christian heritage.

In the Greek Commonwealth, based somewhat on a slave economy, he points out, "this antithesis shaped the entire economy. It appraised labor and production as mean and servile, leisure and consumption as noble and free. Aristotle speaks of the slave as a tool with life in it, and of a tool as a lifeless slave. He looks upon people who work with their hands as incapable of the dignity and worth proper to free men, by nature unable to perceive the truth of things because unable to participate in the consummatory delights of a well-prepared meal, of well-played music, and of aptly reasoned ideas."

No reference is made by the author to the fact that the Greek sculptors, by the work of their own hands in the Periclean heyday of the Athenian community, created some of the noblest representations of the human form and gave expression to some of the noblest structures of the human spirit.

Across the centuries, he points out, has also come, with Biblical power, the voice of Jehovah in the Garden of Eden, saying to Adam, "Because thou has eaten of the tree, of which I commanded thee, saying: *Thou shalt not eat of it:* cursed is the ground for thy sake . . . in toil shalt thou eat of it all the days of thy life; . . . in the sweat of thy face shalt thou eat bread until thou return unto the ground."

In consideration of the influence and expressions of the Hebraic-Christian tradition in the development of the separation of culture from vocation, might have been cited, on the other hand, the counter-examples of Jesus, the carpenter, who projected his workaday life into a concern for spiritual preparation of places in his Father's house in which there were many mansions; Peter, the fisherman, who became the fisher of men; and Paul, the tentmaker, who plied his trade as a way of living in his evangelism for a way of life. Also might have been cited the medieval monks who dignified labor in their assignments of work by hand as part of the daily regimen of monastic life.

By implication only is there recognition of the values of the members of the medieval guilds as skilled and devout craftsmen in the building of the cathedrals which still tower from their medieval foundations across the centuries into modern times as among the noblest creations of the human hand and human spirit. The medieval artisans with their creations of hand, mind and spirit, with their plays and music in religious ceremonies and civic enterprises, are one of the sources in the development of the synthesis of vocation and culture. These craft and merchant guildsmen, with their industrial, commercial and cultural integration and enterprises, played their part in the rise of medieval towns, looking toward the urbanization of civilization, the rise of the middle class, the expansion of trade in the high adventures of exploration and discovery in the great Commercial Revolution, and in the efflorescence of the human spirit called the Renaissance—recovering the ancient classical culture, fulfilling the later medieval age and inaugurating modern times.

In their reciprocal intercultural relations, I may observe, the coming Industrial Revolution was made necessary by the Commercial Revolution and was made possible by the Scientific Revolution, which followed upon the Renaissance. Yet both the synthesis of vocation and culture made by the medi-

eval craftsman and the plural culture, increasingly characteristic of the Renaissance man, got submerged or lost in the ac-
cumulation and specialization of knowledge, the subdivision of
labor, the interchangeability of mechanical parts, the assembly
lines and mass machine production of our later modern times.
It is not only the increasing submergence or the elimination
of the skilled craftsman, who put himself into the wholeness
of his creation, but also the loss of the synthesis of vocation
and culture, that are made vivid in the analysis of Professor
Kallen.

He goes on to say further, regarding the separation of culture from vocation and the consequent conception of "culture" that "culture so taken and pursued is a cut-flower
culture. It is a sensitive plant doomed to fade early and perish
even in the most hydroponic gentleman of culture and refinement, for it is a terminal product cut off from its roots as well
as its soil, and therefore kept alive by only artificial means.
. . . Also as our own times are aware, as early ones were not,
that culture cannot be segregated from vocation and live any-
more than the 'consumption' of the economist can continue
independent of 'production.'"

Along with the development of a "cut-flower" culture are
compensatory developments and forces which are part of the
promise and hope of contemporary American culture and
democracy. Professor Kallen observes that the "transposition
(of the industrial worker) from the level of a machine part to
the level of a community is often accomplished by means of
a trade-union."

Anyone, like myself, however opposed to a government-
compelled union shop, who had the privilege of hearing the
late and widely lamented Philip Murray, in a plea before the
National Defense Mediation Board in "the captive mines" case,
speak of the place of the miner's union in the life of the miner's
family and the mining community could but realize that the
labor-union is a vitally real part of the miner's life, the miner's
culture and the hopes of his wife and children, their conditions of life and labor, their social and political activities and
their integration into the life of their whole community.

The self-organization of industrial workers in labor-unions
for co-operation and for collective bargaining is the means by

which they have a share in determining the terms of their labor, the conditions of their life and the hopes of their children.

The rise of the labor-union, I may add, following in the train of the successive stages of the autonomous organization of people in churches, parliaments, and corporations, is one of the latest chapters in the struggle for human liberty in the rise of democracy in the modern world. Through the labor-union the industrial workers pass from the mechanically automatic and daily repetitive work of the assembly lines into increasingly equal and lively participation in the processes, the life and the culture of the community, the state, the nation and the world, of which they are an increasingly vital, dynamic and organic part.

In his later analysis of the interrelation of cultural pluralism and the American Idea, Professor Kallen observes that industrialization, as an evolving factor "in the diversification of the economy with its manifold new occupations reënforced the process" of their interrelation. "Each industry generates a characteristic re-grouping of individuals already in union with many others in a multitude of ways. Each plant has a specific configuration of thoughts, tools and things with its own specific science and art, couched in a characteristic terminology or dialect, that becomes the stuff of a new tradition and that newer fellow workers take over from the older ones and pass on to the still newer ones. Each occupation in due course gives rise to characters, fables, symbols, capable of imaginative projection as tale, poem or picture of the sort that keeps recurring in the periodical literature and every so often enter signally into the wider stream of national expression. This process is an orchestration of diverse utterances of diversities—regional, local, religious, ethnic, esthetic, industrial, sporting and political—each developing freely and characteristically in its own enclave and somehow so interfused with the others, as to suggest, even to symbolize, the dynamic of the whole. Each is a culture reservoir whence flows its own singularity of expression to unite in the concrete intercultural total which is the culture of America."

Further in consideration of the impact of industrialism on the culture of America, culture considered as the group culture embracing the total economy of their life together, Pro-

fessor Kallen might have observed that there is now a further
lessening of the antithesis between vocation and culture made
possible by the shorter hours of work won by labor-unions
for scores of millions of American workers. The Industrial
Revolution in its first socially uncontrolled phase, which re-
sulted in low wages and inhumanly long and exhausting hours
of work, provided little basis and left little vitality and no time
for the projection of culture from vocation, or the integration
of vocation and culture, or the development of the total personality.

Mass production, higher wages and shorter hours of work
in the later phase of the Industrial Revolution, it is increasingly
true to observe, make possible for increasing millions of the
workers, increasing leisure. Shorter hours, higher wages and
increasing leisure, not only emancipate the human body from
wage slavery but also liberate the human personality for a
more total culture of the body, mind and spirit of scores of
millions of American workers now increasingly devoted to
education, recreation, community life, national and international affairs. Assembly lines and mass production of modern industrialism, with all their limitations and frustrations,
make possible the nobler use of a higher leisure, creatively and
recreatively, by the people in fairer sharing of the frustrations,
aspirations and struggles of democracy toward the good life
of the great society.

II. THE IMPACT ON AMERICAN CULTURAL PLURALISM OF THE
THREATS AND PRESSURES OF TOTALITARIAN TYRANNY AND
AGGRESSION FROM WITHOUT AND FOR CONFORMITY AND UNI-
FORMITY FROM WITHIN

A greater menace to American cultural pluralism than modern industrialism, mass assembly lines and mass production, I
would agree, was recently Fascist, and is now Communist
totalitarianism. The pressures and aggressions of the Communist police state from without and the subversions and fears
of the international Communist conspiracy from within, combined to induce for a time counter pressures and aggressions
against freedom of the mind, freedom of association and cultural pluralism, in incipient steps toward the absolute conformity, uniformity and mediocrity of the totalitarian police

state. The overriding demands and power of conformity and security were subjugating the very values and hazards of freedom without which there can be neither enduring security nor real progress. This fear of real subversion and actual disloyalty carried over into a fear of dissent from and nonconformity with what powerful, privileged, reactionary and some sincerely conservative and patriotic groups considered the established and rightful ways of the *status quo*. The *status quo* of these groups became identified with loyal Americanism. Decent Americans were mustered against honest dissent, wholesome nonconformity and free association of people devoted to carrying forward the ideas and programs of historic Americanism in fulfillment of its principles of the equal freedom and opportunity of all people regardless of race, religion, color, creed, or economic status. Totalitarian threats and pressures from within and without intensify, as Kallen says, that sense of insecurity arising from "whatever differs from the selves of heritage and habit we struggle 'to preserve.' The difference evokes at least uneasiness which may mount to anxiety, to fear, to rage. We have to learn to acquiesce in change for our faiths and works and to overcome our disposition to appraise such change in others as breach of faith and deficiency of character, unless it confronts our own diversification with no challenge but surely confirms our views and values by conforming to them. . . . Sometimes we protect ourselves by ostracizing the different, sometimes by coercing, indenturing or enslaving, sometimes by liquidating it. . . . An imperialism of the mind (as witnessed in the recent history by Fascist Germany, Communist Russia and Falangist Spain) is projected (or attempted as in the recent history of the United States) and a cultural colonialism set up, both postulated in power to impose on the diverse conformation or servitude."

Kallen hopefully observes, regarding this second menace to cultural pluralism and the American Idea, that . . . "on the whole and in the long run such imperialisms win only battles, not wars. No institution of any civilization ever gathers enough power to impose an everlasting submission and servitude upon the different or to suppress differentiation within the same. Every authoritarian culture, hence, has its perennial spyings and inquisitions and purges, and every non-authoritarian culture seeks them on occasion, witness mccarthyism in mid-century United States."

One of the sources of freedom against totalitarian conformity and authoritarian culture and one of the perennial springs of the cultural pluralism of the American Idea is the wholesome disposition of Americans to form, join, disband or continue associations in causes and movements rooted in their historic heritage and dear to their humane hopes of equal liberties and opportunity for all people. Says Kallen, "Among free people most such associations are what we call mobility, they form, change, grow, dissolve, at the option of individuals who constitute them, and are creations of their consent."

Free associations in worthy causes become the special objectives for subversive infiltration. The test of the loyalty of the overwhelming majority of the members, who had joined an association in good faith was not the purpose of the few, who, it later appeared joined with ulterior design. The real test was in the resolutions, programs and activities actually adopted by the overwhelming majority for the freedom and equal opportunity of all people in the best American tradition. In those associations in which the humane American line overwhelmingly prevailed, fellow traveling, if any, was not by the great majority which held and advanced the line of their American heritage and humane hopes. It would constitute an ironical picture if some members of the small infiltrating minority sought through guilt by association to smear members of the majority who overwhelmingly defeated them on the merits of issues and struggles involving condemnation of totalitarian aggressions against both the civil liberties of individuals and the independence of small nations. Against possible future infiltration and subversion the associations involved could either bar to membership any totalitarian who sought to use civil liberties for the destruction of freedom or simply bring to an end that association itself and seek expression and find channels for action in other or new associations barred to known subversives. Those who covertly sought to prostitute freedom to subversion could find no reasonable ground for their rage against either the denial of membership to them or the ending of the life of an association which their designs could not control but could in effect destroy by causing the overwhelming majority to end the association altogether. Nevertheless, the principle of free association survives and carries on in the persistent and wholesome habit of the American people, in spite of all abuses, to exercise the precious freedom of private initiative of the citizen and his voluntary association in humane causes. Kallen says in this connection: "His safety is their numbers; his freedom is their diversity. The more of them he can join or leave, the more varied their form and function, the more abundant . . . [etc.] is likely to be the personality which lives and moves and nourishes its being among the diverse communions and thus orchestrates a growing pluralism of association into the wholeness of his individuality."

This growing pluralism of association cannot be crushed under anxious pressures and imposed conformities induced by the fear of the stigma of guilt by association or the fantastic application of "security risk" to Americans who have spent their lives and risked hazards of career and reputation in their undaunted struggles for a larger fulfillment of the heritage and hope of the American dream. For this American Idea, this freedom of association and this cultural pluralism, millions of Americans crossed the oceans, east and west, in their own defense and in the collective self-defense and advancement of the equal freedom, opportunity, well-being and peace of all people. They still would work and struggle for an America and a world in which it would not be necessary to cross oceans again except in friendship, reciprocal trade and cultural exchange.

Professor Kallen goes on to say that "Florian Znaniecki, renewing Mazzini for today, observes that 'a solidly human collectivity of hundreds, of thousands, even millions of people who share the same culture can exist for a time without a common political government' . . . that 'national cultural societies' are found in many lands, he argues, indicates that politics is not enough, that cultures are essential, that world peace can come only as the world's people unite into a 'world culture society' creating a 'world culture.' F. C. S. Northrop underscores the observation that 'it is culturism rather than nationalism that is the rising fact in the world today,' and that the road to peace is the role of cultural parity developing in an intercultural co-operation that should provide a passage from western colonialism and Asiatic revolt," and thus seek to avoid the road to another war with its possible destruction of the accumulated cultures of the world.

The way for the survival of the human race is more in the freedom of cultural pluralism and the free and creative co-operation of nations in an organically growing and more effective United Nations than in the tyranny and sterility of the monolithic culture of the totalitarian world police state. Liberation is not in *Proletcult*, the cult of the Proletarians of Eden and Cedar Paul, as Professor Kallen says: "They projected *Proletcult* as a fighting culture aiming at the overthrow of capitalism and at the replacement of democratic culture and bourgeois ideology with ergocratic culture and proletarian ideology. . . . They were excited by what they had heard and read about the Bolshevik Revolution in Russia, like the Sidney Webbs taking its pretensions for performance, its words for events . . . that their ergocratic culture and pro-letarian ideology were but symbols and slogans of the Lenin-Stalinist march through blood and death to power, the Prolet-cultists' enamored faith could neither note nor concede. Nor could they recognize that personality images, which chan-nelled workingmen's ambitions and desires, were still the forms of force, freedom and fulfillment that tradition com-municated and the neighborhood supplied.

"These, also the hierarchies of Kremlin Commissars took over, willy-nilly, from bourgeois opposite numbers. Dress, diet, comforts, protocols, housing, transportation, entertain-ment—in everything but manners—they emulate the ruling hierarchies of the condemned 'bourgeois' world. In manners they emulate the vituperative rudeness which is the signature of their Proletcult. It contrasts sharply, not only with the amenities of intercourse of the 'bourgeois,' but also with the traditional courtesy of the Russian peoples and of all simple peoples whose working and living are so interdependent. . . . But, in order to vindicate the ruthless and bloody translocation of power, to defend its privileged beneficiaries from their over-throw (and prevent the resurgence of free associations and cultural pluralism) a sadistic policing of all forms of associa-tions was installed and was rationalized by forbidding or eradi-cating the symbols and images of the traditional culture, rigidly censoring opinion, the arts and the sciences into conformity with the creed and code of *Proletcult*.

"In *1984*, George Orwell stripped naked its logic and logistic; the foregone conclusion that every totalitarian ruler, secular Big Brother or sacerdotal Holy Father, must overtly or covertly assume infallibility in order to rationalize his irrational authority. . . . Its task is constantly to alter the records of the past so that they suit the changing practices of the power-holders as they act in such wise as to stay in power. Their directive is the apothegm: *Who controls the past controls the future; who controls the present controls the past.*

"Proletcult, it will be seen, whether as aspiration or achievement, perpetuates the invidious distinction between culture and vocation intrinsic to the tradition but dresses it up in different images and symbols and encodes it in different parables."

The world of freedom and cultural pluralism on guard, it may pertinently be observed, against the designs and wiles of totalitarian infiltration and without confusing the honest dissent of cultural pluralism with the real disloyalty of cultural totalitarianism, must meantime be strong not only in the basic and creative liberties of dynamic democracy but also must be strong in national defense and collective security against the combined power of monolithic cultural tyranny, unresting subversion and ruthless aggression. The American people, thus strong in the faith of their own historic liberties and humane hopes can, in competitive service in widening the areas of international co-operation for a more productive life east and west, peacefully advance the faith, power and humane values of freedom, cultural pluralism and dynamic democracy.

In competitive existence and widening, through the United Nations and its Specialized Agencies, the areas of international co-operation for freedom, well-being, justice and peace, the American people, and all free peoples, thus collectively strong in the faith of their historic liberties and humane hopes, may become spiritual participants in, and peacefully victorious witnesses of, the disintegration of the totalitarian police state. Its recession will come with the rising well-being of the people, the human will to freedom and the resurgence of cultural pluralism from within the productive life, the dynamic energies, the democratic impulses and humane hopes of the people themselves for a fairer, freer, friendlier and more creative life for all.

III. CULTURAL PLURALISM IMPLICIT IN THE AMERICAN IDEA

The American Idea, it must be acknowledged, has at times been discolored, checkmated and even betrayed by its involvement with Alien and Sedition Laws, slavery, Know-Nothingism, Ku Kluxism, economic exploitation, McCarthyism, racism and colonialism. More authentic and enduring are the examples and principles of the American Revolution and the American War Between the States.

In the eloquent address opening the Bandung Conference of Asian-African people, President Soekarno took significant note of the fact that the very day of its opening was the 180th anniversary of the midnight ride of Paul Revere calling men to arms in the first successful revolt against modern colonialism. The people's revolution is still on the march and the impact of its ideas are still felt around the world. The American Civil War is, as emphasized by Kallen, unique in the titanic struggle of free men for the freedom of men not free.

Carrying on above and beyond the demands for the fearsome conforming of 100 per-cent pseudo-Americanism are the remembered hazards of freedom on Roanoke, at Jamestown, Plymouth Rock, New Amsterdam, the Jerseys, New Sweden, on the Ashley River and on the Savannah; the religious freedom of Rhode Island, Maryland and Pennsylvania, the sayings of Poor Richard; the advance resolves for Independence by North Carolina and Virginia; the Virginia Statute of Religious Liberty and Bill of Rights; the Declaration of Independence; Tom Paine's *Common Sense* and *The Crisis;* the character of George Washington, the rock of the Revolution, upon whom broke defeat, intrigue, despair, as he fathered the birth of a nation for freeing the earth in time; the Northwest Ordinance; the Constitution; the Monroe Doctrine; Webster's Apostrophe to the meaning of the Flag; the writings of Jefferson, Emerson, Thoreau, Theodore Parker and Walt Whitman and the speeches of Lincoln; the Emancipation Proclamation; the Gettysburg Address; the Civil War Amend-

ments; Lincoln's magnanimity in victory; Lee's spirit of recon-
ciliation and the sublimity of his duties in defeat; the Granger
Movement; the Labor Movement; the Woman's Movement;
the humanitarian crusades; the western progressivism of Bryan
and La Follette, the risen South of Henry Grady, J. L. M.
Curry, Booker T. Washington, Edgar Gardner Murphy, Ed-
win A. Alderman, Charles D. McIver and Charles B. Aycock;
the Square Deal of Theodore Roosevelt; the New Freedom of
Woodrow Wilson, the Fourteen Points and the League of
Nations; the epochal peaceful revolution of the manifold New
Deal of Franklin D. Roosevelt, the Atlantic Charter; the
Charter of the United Nations; the Fair Deal of Harry S.
Truman; the Truman Doctrine, the Marshall Plan and the
Point-Four Program; the Universal Declaration of Human
Rights; the Decision of the Supreme Court against legal segre-
gation; and President Eisenhower's Atoms for Peace and the
spirit of Geneva.

The American Idea and Cultural Pluralism, with its One and
the Many, monism and pluralism, federalism and states' rights,
collectivism and individualism, the liberty of the individual
and the security of the nation, are postulated in:

I. One God, many religions and various denominations with
a common devotion to the universal faith of the Fatherhood
of one God and the brotherhood of all people.

The World Parliament of communicants of the Hindu,
Buddhist, Parsee, Taoist, Shintoist, Jewish, Islamic and Christian religions, is based on mutual respect and tolerance in the
common conception of the moral sovereignty which under-
girds the nature of the universe and the life and destiny of
man.

In expression of the inward spiritual urge, in the need and
yearning for love, justice and mercy, in the unfolding of
men's consciousness of God and His infinite love, in the sense
of man's inadequacy, and in the realization of the higher self
in other selves, great religions and ethical systems developed
among people in wide regions in the East and West. The West
is in debt to the East as the birthplace of all the great religions.
Above profound differences and anachronisms in the upward
reach for truth, goodness and beauty, there emerged and survived, as treasures of the spirit, ethical principles common to

Judaism, Zoroastrianism, Hinduism, Confucianism, Taoism, Shintoism, Buddhism, Stoicism, Islam, and Christianity.

The cultures cradled on the Nile, between the Euphrates and the Tigris, in the Indo-Gangetic Plain and Peninsular India, between Yangtze Kiang and the Hwang Ho, in the Graeco-Roman world, in Islam across the middle of the earth from the Atlantic to Indonesia, and in the Mediterranean-European-American West, became in their interaction and organic growth the substance and process of the civilization of the past which lives in the present. The Upanishads and Bhaga-vad-Gita of the Hindus, the Zend Avesta of the Parsees, the ethical sayings of Confucius, the humane teachings of Buddha, the Koran of Muhammud, the Stoic philosophy of the Greeks and Romans, the Bible of the Jews and the teachings and spiritual mission of the Jesus of history and the Christ of faith, all belong to the community of faith. Moses, Ashoka, Socrates, Saint Francis, Florence Nightingale, Abraham Lincoln, Pasteur, Tolstoi, Sun Yat Sen and Gandhi express the universality of the dignity of man, the moral law, the noble aspirations of the human spirit and the humane capacities and the spiritual faith of our common humanity.

As a basic foundation of the cultural pluralism implicit in the American Idea are the spiritual legacies of peoples, East and West, and the Judaic-Christian-classical-patristic-scholastic-humanistic-scientific-industrial-democratic-heritage of the West.

Balanced against religious wars, tyrannies, bigotries, inquisitions, persecutions, sanctions of injustice, betrayals and frustrations, are the churches' spiritual satisfactions, moral idealism, and humane ministrations to the sufferings, needs and hopes of people in their everyday life. Their deeper communions in the conception of the Fatherhood of one God and the brotherhood of all people have been mankind's chief resource in the struggle for freedom and democracy. In wide meaning and the long run churches have been among the most beneficent institutions in Western history.

The National Conference of Christians and Jews is an expression of the pluralism of our Hebraic-Christian heritage.

The spiritual co-operation of Jews, Catholics and Protestants is an expression of the values of cultural pluralism not only without the surrender of any conviction but rather with an invigoration of the meaning of each faith. From the Jews came the high conception of one God, the sovereignty of the moral law, the greatest book and the greatest life in history, and the progressive revelation of God in the experience of a great people. The old and the new prophets of Judaism still speak for personal goodness and against social injustice with a spiritual power which exalts the moral wisdom of a hundred generations above the sophistication of any one generation. Judaism, the foundation of the world religions, Christianity and Islam, is one of the sanctuaries of the spirit for the triumph of the moral law over the economic, political and cultural tyranny of the police state.

It was the Catholics, who, from Judaic foundations, carried across Europe to America and the world the message of the incarnation of the love of God in Jesus and his universal compassion for the redemption of all men. The sackable city of Rome became the unsackable City of God. The little congregation of lowly believers, unbroken in faith, triumphed over ostracism, dungeons, torture and the beasts of the arena, and grew into the Church Universal as the spiritual refuge of heroism and hope of the people in dark times. Amid the disintegration of the empire, the medieval church tutored the barbarians of the north, necessarily at a level much lower than the level of the ancient classical learning. Cultural ascent was made from the Dark Ages to the Scholastic Synthesis to the Renaissance to modern science. Within the Catholic domains developed the parliaments, the cathedrals and the universities, towering across the centuries as diverse expressions of the manifold faith and culture of the modern world. The ministers and missions of compassion and mercy carry the cross far and near in its call to brotherhood and heroism in the sharing and giving of life. Spiritual Catholicism is an inner fortress of the spirit against Fascist and Communist totalitarianism in the present world.

The Protestants, in their protests and then in their revolt against abuses in the Church, gave to the cultural pluralism of the West and to the American Idea an emphasis in the right of private judgment. This freedom of the individual, in his direct communion with God, added to the sense of human unworthiness and humility in the presence of God one of dignity and equality as a child of God in the brotherhood of all people, without the intermediation of bishop or king or the councils of men.

Luther's ninety-five theses nailed on the church door at Wittenberg, his refusal, with his life at stake, to recant his individual interpretation, and his declaration at the imperial Diet of Worms, "Here I stand so help me God, I can do no other," were birth cries of Protestantism.

Plymouth Rock, in 1620, became one of the foundation stones of a new nation. Congregationalism contributed to the meaning of town meetings and local self-government. The federalism of congregations, presbyteries, synods and general assemblies contributed to the federalism of the Republic. The Anglican growers of crops on the banks of the James River in old Virginia, in order to bargain collectively with the London Company, organized the first representative assembly in the New World, which became one of those foundations of democracy which still flies its flag free in the modern world.

In many forms Protestantism spread across Western and Northern Europe, the American states and the British dominions, with a spiritual dynamic and democratic value imperiled around the earth today. The "dissidence of dissent" which was the eloquent appreciation by Edmund Burke of the American spirit of liberty, is still a spiritual resource of freedom in our time.

Judaism, Catholicism and Protestantism, as different expressions of the vigor and variety of the multi-cultural spiritual heritage, have in their great Hebraic-Christian-Graeco-Roman-Medieval-European-scholastic-modern-renascent-national-scientific-democratic-federal-American pluralism, a common cause, under God, in the manifold purposes of the United Nations for human freedom, brotherhood and peace on earth in the community of the faiths of the family of man.

II. One universe and many various interpretations: animistic, theological, deistic, mechanistic, materialistic, vitalistic, energetic and spiritual.

By astronomy the earth has been dethroned as the center of the universe and has become one of the smaller planets of one of the smaller stars among millions of larger stars of one galaxy of stars among millions of galaxies of stars in the expanding universe.

The mechanistic theory of the universe, man and the self-balancing economic system, the theory of biological evolution, the economic interpretation of history, the behavioristic theory of human psychology, and the subjection of reason to the power of the subconscious mind, deep in the nature and inheritance of man, all combined to dethrone the earth as the center of the universe, man as a special creation four thousand years ago, the economic system as self-perfecting, and human reason as exalted in its independence. By biology and geology man has been identified as an animal in the evolution of life from the lowest to the highest species.

But this theory of the physical descent of man from lower species is accompanied by the spiritual conception of the ascent of man in the image of God and revealed in the human experience and moral law of the Jewish people and incarnate in the Jesus of history and the Christ of faith, personally redemptive, socially regenerative and spiritually creative, who would have all people become more truly the children of God and the brothers of all, in the equal freedom, dignity and opportunity of the great adventure of the human pilgrimage toward the Kingdom of God who "made of one blood all the nations of men for to dwell on the face of the earth."

III. One United Nations and sixty member nations, free and sovereign, independent and interdependent, with a goal of universal membership for all nations in accordance with the Charter of the United Nations.

In the political evolution of states from city-states to empire-states to feudal-states to nation-states, modern science and technology have made available potentialities for either global concentration of the will to absolute power or co-operation of nations in the use of scientific power, humane knowledge and the impulse to love, create and share. Increasingly, in the minds, work and prayers of the people, the next transition of states would not be from the nation-states to a totalitarian world police state, but rather to the more effective co-operation of nation-states in a more adequate United Nations in the more inclusive collective security of freedom, justice, well-being, compassion and peace of all people.

IV. One World, composite of the American-European democratic world, the British Commonwealth of Nations, the totalitarian Soviet-Chinese and satellite Communist world, the Neutralist world, the Islamic world, the Asian, Pacific and African worlds, overlapping and interlocking in the cross-currents of democratic liberties, collective totalitarianism, collective self-defense of freedom, and independent neutralism, with security and interdependence deriving from the growing strength of the collective security of freedom, justice and peace.

V. One Pan American Union of States. Composed of British, Spanish, Portuguese, French, German, Negro, American Indian, Italian, Jewish, Chinese, Japanese, Greek, Polish, Russian, and other Slavic and Asiatic peoples, who give vigor and variety to the racial and cultural pluralism of the Americas.

The Monroe Doctrine of the United States, which for a century and a quarter unilaterally guaranteed the freedom and independence of Latin American nations, has been supplanted by the Pact of Rio, based on the multilateral and mutual cooperation and interdependence of the twenty-one American nations.

VI. One United States and Forty-eight States: *e pluribus unum*, a union of states and a nation of people; dualism, federalism, separation of powers, local, state and federal, legislative, executive and judicial; the pluralism of regions, races, colors, creeds, nationalities, and cultures; a manifold social-capitalism and a balanced and various economy of private and public enterprise; a vast continent fronting the two great oceans, east and west, between the old world and the new; a frontier people in possession of the most abundant resources ever entrusted to any people, plural heirs of all great cultures of mankind unfolding in the fresh and various freedoms of a cultural pluralism, inherited from the living past, indigenous in its various rootage, original in its composite freshness and organic in the growth of the American Idea as a part of the vigor and variety of the democratic impulses and the humane hopes of all people in their high adventure toward the Kingdom of God, in whose spiritual house are many mansions of freedom and hope for the family of man.

DR. KALLEN'S IDEA OF AMERICANISM
AND CULTURAL RELATIVISM

by R. J. Henle, S.J.

Dean, St. Louis University Graduate School

It would obviously be impossible, in so short a paper, to deal with the full reach of Doctor Kallen's fine exposition. With much of it I agree, but there is one point of disagreement which appears to me to be of very significant importance. To this point I will direct my attention.

A salient feature of American society is its extraordinary cultural diversity, a diversity which displays itself in differences of theology and philosophy, of race, religion, culture and national origins.

The political problem for such a society is that of attaining a basic national unity, an internal peace and harmony so that the political society can maintain and promote, within its proper sphere of activity, a genuine common good. It is obvious, surely, that no substantial peace and no effective harmony can be attained except by an agreement of minds. Yet to demand an agreement of minds is precisely to destroy the factual diversity and to make of the political power a potential persecutor. Internal strife would be inevitable, for men will fight and die for that which they hold to be true and ultimately necessary.

The problem is, therefore, to respect the diversity while achieving a unity. The American solution to this problem constitutes a unique contribution to political and social theory and practice and is one of the greatest achievement of American practicality, fairness and ingenuity.[1]

[1] R. J. Henle, "American Principles and Religious Schools," *Saint Louis University Law Journal*, Vol. 3, No. 2, 1954; Charles Donahue, "Freedom and Education: The Pluralistic Background," *Thought*, Vol. 27, 1952, pp. 542-560.

The first condition for the solution is the removal of the political unit and its police power from the area of ultimate ideologies.[2] If the government rested on the acceptance as such of a given ideology, or if its power, direct or indirect, made for the repression or the favored survival of any ideology, the pattern of diversity could not be respected. Since the ultimate ideologies of the original colonies were mainly religious in character, this separation was achieved in effect by the Bill of Rights and especially by the First Amendment. Thus the possibility of a political tie-up between a church or sect or religious ideology and the political (at first federal) government was removed from the start. The political society thereby renounced the attributes of a church, became strictly non-ideological and declared itself incompetent in the area of theology and ultimate ideologies. Thus ideologies as such, religious convictions as such are beyond the cognizance of the state; and, consequently, the individuals and institutions embodying them stand before the state as free and equal.

However, this is not yet enough. A purely negative attitude, an ignoring of ideologies in politics, law and civic matters would in practice result in an opposition to them.[3] In dealing with its citizens the state must so take into account the religious and ideological differences as to remain "open" to the diversities presented by different individuals and different institutions. This means that in concrete situations where the interests and activities of the state entwine into a single complex with individual ideologies the position of the state must be adjustable to these ideologies so as truly to maintain the maximum freedom for diversity. This openness has been largely maintained by a series of uniquely ingenious devices and has become our traditional approach to such problems.[4]

[2] By an ultimate ideology I mean a man's convictions about the fundamental meaning of the world and of human life. For a religious person, this coincides, at least in part, with his religious convictions. See also Charles Donahue, "Freedom and Education: the Sacral Problem," *Thought*, Vol. 28, 1953, pp. 209-233.

[3] Cf. *Everson* v. *Board of Education*, 330 U.S. 1 (1947); Cushman, "Public Support of Religious Education in American Constitutional Law," *Illinois Law Review*, Vol. 45, 1950, p. 348.

[4] For example: the acceptance of a minister, priest or rabbi as a civil official in the marriage ceremony, *depending upon* the choice of the individuals to be married. Likewise, the arrangements for court testimony, the Chaplains'

In all such cases, however, the state makes no judgment about the validity or truth of the conscience of the individual or his sincerely accepted ideology. It merely accepts that which the individual holds and ratifies the resulting arrangement, not because it involves Lutheran or Jewish or Catholic or secularist ideas but because it protects the *positive* freedom of the individual mind and conscience.

In effect, then, the establishment of such a political unit separates the state from the society in which it functions and even from a majority within that society. For the very condition of success in such a political undertaking is that the state maintain the same openness to minority ideologies as majority ones. Thus the courts have, in a series of decisions, protected the rather unpopular positions of the Jehovah's Witnesses. This implies no official decision with regard to the ideology of the Jehovah's Witnesses; it means that, as citizens, their complete freedom is to be protected as far as possible.

When we turn to the society for which such a political framework has been constructed, we find that diversity in ultimate convictions is again mediated by individual consciences and accepted by others not in itself but as the expression of the sincere convictions of individuals. Thus the Lutheran accepts the Catholic, the Jew, the secularist, not because he agrees with their ultimate ideologies or because he thinks the differences of religious belief are of no consequence but because he respects the sincerity and convictions of others. From the standpoint of the content of the convictions, he may firmly believe that the Catholic, the Jew and the secularist are fundamentally wrong in matters of the greatest importance and he may use every means within his power to persuade them to accept what to him is a view much better than theirs, perhaps of decisive importance for their lives. Moreover, he may be convinced that wide acceptance of Christianity or even of Lutheranism within American society is necessary for the continuation of the kind of freedom and the kind of society we now have. All these views become simultaneously possible within the framework of the American pattern—an ingenious outcome of the American solution. The Lutheran

Corps, orphans, the educational G.I. benefits, etc. See R. J. Henle, "American Principles and Religious Schools." *Op. cit.*

may refuse, because of religious differences, to marry a Catholic; he may belong to a church which excludes and excommunicates those who think as Catholics or as Unitarians. All this is simply to say that he may be fully and freely a convinced Lutheran without in any way rendering his Americanism suspect or less "orthodox." Thus the American solution is precisely one which solves the problem of diversity by granting the full range of personal and institutional freedoms requisite for it.

The American solution, then, embodies these policy decisions: (1) The state is non-ideological; it cannot either oppose or develop a specific ideology; (2) Every citizen can be wholly and completely a citizen and a member of American society while being at the same time wholly and consistently a member of a given church, a believer in a given ideology; (3) Individual persons, despite differences, are to be respected and accorded full rights. This attitude of acceptance rests on a distinction between the person with his free conscience and the content of his belief which may be denied and rejected.

Americanism therefore consists of a set of practical political and social policies and attitudes. These do not add up to another ultimate ideology; rather, in view of the diversity of the American tradition and of present thought, they lie open to a grounding by different Americans in different ultimate principles.[5] Thus a Catholic may see them as an expression of Christian love and as the prudential working out of the rights of conscience,[6] a Liberal may view them as the best practical

[5] What I mean in speaking of an "openness" with regard to ultimate ideologies may be illustrated by a simple example. Three men may agree in condemning discrimination based on race and may energetically work together against it; yet one may see it as a violation of the Christian law of love, another as a violation of a natural law, the third may reject law and love and see it as the only practical way of maintaining peace. If they insisted on unity of ultimate explanation before acting in concert, they would never act; yet in acting together on a practical policy, they do not violate their own ultimate principles.

Dr. Kallen very clearly recognizes that this "openness" has existed historically in the American tradition.

[6] For such a theoretical development see "Troisième Parties," *Tolerance et Communaute Humaine* (various authors), Paris, Casterman, 1952, pp. 107-235; the address of Pope Pius XII to the National Convention of the Italian Catholic Union of Jurists, Rome, December 6, 1953: Gustave Weigel, S.J., "Religious Toleration in a World Society," *America*, 1954, Ch. 90, pp. 375-

means for a maximum of human development. In other words, Americanism is ideologically multivalent, and for this reason it is possible for different groups to incorporate the American outlook into their own pattern of religious and philosophical beliefs.[7]

But Americanism, in so far as it is the *common possession of all of us*, cannot be a common ultimate ideology, since its very essence is to remain open to different ideologies; it cannot be a surrogate for a religion or be reduced to a simple and uniform "mystique."

Moreover, an American may be convinced that a certain ideology is not only untrue and mistaken but is a serious threat to the pattern of Americanism itself, while at the same time maintaining that the police power and propaganda forces of the government may not be marshalled against it. Thus one may believe firmly as I do that, if Communistic or secularistic ideologies were to dominate our *society*, the freedoms I have been discussing and our form of government would ultimately collapse, and true human goods would be outlawed, while, at the same time, maintaining, as I do, that the government may act against such ideologies only when they are translated into overt acts or conspiracies against the government or the nation as a whole. By a seeming paradox, a government like ours, which has renounced ideological competence, cannot defend itself at the level of ideologies; it must leave this defense to the free institutions and individuals within its society. It is placed in this difficult position by its very nature and any attempt to change this position would destroy its essential character.[8]

An American need not then believe that all types of diversity are really good things. On the contrary, it is an essential part of Americanism that he be free, without attaint to his Americanism, to reject and condemn ideologies held by other

---

376; John Courtney Murray, S.J., *Governmental Repression of Heresy*, The Catholic Theological Society of America.

[7] Protestant: Samuel Enoch Stumpf, *Democracy and the Christian Faith*, Vanderbilt University, 1950; Jewish: Morris M. Feuerlicht, *Judaism's Influence in the Founding of the Republic*, The Tract Commission, Merchants Building, Cincinnati; Catholic: James Milton O'Neill, *Catholicism and American Freedom*, New York, Harper & Bros., 1952.

[8] Etienne Gilson, *The Breakdown of Morals and Christian Education*, Toronto, Saint Michael's College.

Americans. He may believe that it should be better if all Americans accepted the scientific theory of medicine (i.e. if Christian Science would disappear) or if all would accept Catholicism (i.e. if Protestantism and Judaism were to disappear). His Americanism remains intact as long as he respects the individuals who maintain the diversity and their rights, and uses reason and persuasion to propagate his views.[9]

Full freedom for diversity implies not only the right [10] to be different from one's fellow Americans but the right to hold that one's own views are better and significantly so than another's and the right to criticize, attack, discuss, persuade, provided (1) one does not, simply on the basis of such difference, refuse equal political, civic and common social rights to others, and provided (2) the criticism is honest, sincere and respectful of individuals.

The point or rather theme in Doctor Kallen's paper which I wish to single out for criticism can now be briefly indicated. There seems to be a tendency in his conception to regard Americanism as an ultimate ideology, to make it a surrogate religion, and to identify it with cultural relativism. This is indicated by the very rhetoric—a rhetoric of religious expression—which he employs, by the designation as un-American of exclusive churches, and by the parity of value, which, in the name of the American Idea, he grants to all cultures and apparently to all elements in them except to firm convictions judging better and worse, right and wrong. If the analysis presented in the body of this paper is correct, any common and general definition of Americanism which identifies it with or implies as its ground relativism in values and knowledge is a self-defeating definition.[11] It creates a new in-group of its own and excludes

---

[9] For an excellent description of this attitude, see Most Reverend John J. Wright, D.D., *Education for an Age of Fear*, Boston, Boston College, 1953, pp. 14-15.

[10] It should be obvious that I am speaking of "rights" within a political society and civil structure. Morally speaking, every human being has a moral duty to seek what is true, to accept what is known to be true, and to act in conformity with it. For the Catholic position see: "Condemnation of Father Leonard Feeney," Sacred Congregation of the Holy Office, *The Catholic Mind*, Vol. 1, No. 1080, 1952, pp. 748-752.

[11] The precise error here is to demand a uniformity of ideology, for this places the "unity" in direct contradiction to the "plurality" and makes a combination of the two impossible. Doctor Kallen's explanation ignores the

from "Americanism" precisely that form of diversity and that freedom of mind which has traditionally been the most important in our society. The initial political renunciation of ideological competence was not an assertion that ideological differences were unimportant or equally valuable or equally valueless. So to interpret it would be to ruin the American solution and to place once again, before the religious conscience, a choice of God *or* Caesar.

Obviously, the American Idea is delicately balanced and requires the most careful distinctions and guarded decisions. Precisely because it maintains both a unity and a pluralism, frictional problems are inevitable and only the utmost of good will, sympathetic understanding and practical prudence will keep it a reality. I fear that Doctor Kallen's interpretation deprives the pluralism—in the crucial area of ideology—of substantial reality and thus by an apparent paradox cultural relativism results in ideological monism.

It is because this point is so fundamental that I have passed over the numerous excellent ideas and positions with which I agree and which Doctor Kallen has so ably presented. If this point were accepted, the most prized of our freedoms would become meaningless and Americanism would be turned into a persecuting pressure, forcing a conformity in philosophical relativism.

essential distinction between "accepting" individual human beings and "approving" their ideas. This distinction makes it possible for a dogmatist like myself to accept a cultural relativist while rejecting cultural relativism. See Etienne Gilson, *Dogmatism and Tolerance*, New Brunswick, N.J., Rutgers University Press, 1952.

SOME THOUGHTS ON CULTURAL

PLURALISM AND THE

AMERICAN IDEA

by Herold C. Hunt

Undersecretary, Department of Health, Education, and Welfare

It is with a definition of culture as the sum of a nation's growth in terms of expression that Kallen works in developing *Cultural Pluralism and the American Idea.* On an interesting and informative account of the cultural growth of America the author builds his concept of an intellectual idea of Americanism. The treatment includes and omits much of America's heritage. It culminates in the view that in such an idea of social growth and human living lies the hope of the world. Although it is easily possible to agree with much that Kallen writes there is a responsibility to point out some omissions and unacceptable assumptions before considering the reality of his conclusion.

Kallen's lengthy account of the various concepts of culture is both interesting and plausible. The balance of his thesis seems to argue for a clear distinction between vocation and culture, work and leisure. While this is not his purpose, he does not make it clear that these are factors which are dependent upon each other. Possibly his concept of work is at fault for he appears to believe that what he calls a traditional distinction between work and leisure, vocation and culture, strongly exists. Views of the beliefs of certain groups of people, especially in the nineteenth century are, however, too often taken to be traditional. Such errors have frequently been made in the area of morals. During the Renaissance for example, with the new learning, individuality was so stressed that the very purpose of life became the cultivation of oneself and of living, instead of being merely a pilgrimage from birth to death. This was in fact work. It was industry. It was realized through one's whole expression and being.

Yet again, Kallen's interpretation of the truth of the myth of the Garden of Eden presents the viewpoint that work was without and leisure within. This is not necessarily so. Another interpretation which might be equally valid could be that work outside was accompanied with pain and toil, while that which was inside was work which was pleasant and agreeable. It was, it will be recalled, the Puritans, who did so much in the founding of America, who lifted the concept of work almost to the level of godliness. Here, possibly, is a view of work and culture which Kallen has not considered.

Does not the average American who seeks life at night, in contrast to work by day, work at his interests, hobbies and tastes? Does not this become his true vocation and the sum total of his expression of his culture? It is unnecessary to labor this point further, however, as it is possible to agree with Kallen's apparent final suggestion that culture depends upon the work and environment of the individual and ultimately the group. It is a result of the accumulative aspects of living, past and present.

Kallen spends much time warning of the ineffectiveness of the natural tendency for groups to seek to establish their felt supremacy. He gives evidence of this "chosen" concept in the Greeks, the Jews and even the totalitarians of only yesterday. The tendency to feel superior to the Barbarians, Gentiles and Non-Aryans is to Kallen a natural tendency of in-group feeling which is never long successful. Again, the example of the Puritans he fails to mention. These people had their chosen and their elect. The elect set rules of behavior and conduct which all others were to follow. The Puritan record of persecution of Quakers, of Roger Williams and others is a revealing example of this desire for oneness and of the rejection of differences. In the heritage of the American people Puritanism has played an important part. Some people see its emphasis on industry (work) and on being thrifty as those factors which have contributed most to the development of the country and the production of its culture. Others find it a restrictive factor, creating in Americans frustrating consciences, differences between expressed beliefs and actions and a tendency to investigate and pry into each other's doings.

It is here that there are deficiencies in Kallen's account of the development of American culture. Curiously enough he does not mention Franklin's words that in this country a man is asked not who he is, but what he can do. This attitude symbolized not only American culture of the early days but also that which is still held as the basis for American democracy, despite the fact that today it is such people as the English working class who proudly proclaim their self-regarded lowly status and not the American middle class. Is there, then, a flight from shirtsleeves by educational and social mobility? How have present-day economics contributed to this? Does everyone want to consume and few produce, even in sports? What is American culture going to conceive of as being the right uses of leisure, which is becoming available in greater degree for almost everyone? These are further questions which Kallen does not answer but which surely belong to a concept of culture.

Kallen sees the whole growth of American expression in its arts, history, literature, economy, and social concepts as culminating in an idea of a way of life. He sees its expression first in the Declaration of Independence without recognizing the sources of it in Locke and the culture of the time. He sees its growth on the frontier without considering the critics who point out that much of the belief in democracy was taken to the frontier by the settlers themselves. He speaks of the Civil War as a war of liberty when its reasons and causes are still debated today. He equates the American Idea to the new racism without mentioning its adverse effects in American nationalism in Cuba and the Philippines. He speaks of the rise of monism and the oneness concept of Americanism without sufficient regard for the political and social conditions of the times which made the quest for unity strong. He speaks of the Ku Klux Klan and other organizations in this regard without sufficient recognition of the fact that the forces towards uniformity which they represent, have always existed in American history. He speaks of the Civil Liberties Movement, the Woman's Movement and the Labor Movement as wholly restricted to the American scene rather than a part of the development of Western civilization. He finally concludes that the American idea which now fully accepts all cultures not as in a melting pot but with mutual and symphonic regard is the hope of the world. It is a way of life which can bring peaceful living and coexistence to the diverse cultures of mankind, Kallen holds.

Why is there a rejection of the word democratic and a substitution of American? Is it to be said that all peoples who believe in liberty and equality and peaceful living are pursuing the "American" idea? What is the difference between Kallen's concept of the American idea and American nationalism, apart from inserting an acceptance of all, in place of making all one? Both are attitudes which exist in the minds of the people. A well-traveled man can arrive home as much a nationalist as ever, rather than an internationalist, if his earlier held opinions are never altered. Similarly with a cultural wanderer. Should a man therefore want to embrace the varying subcultures of his country and his times, and if so, if he is successful does he epitomize the cultured person? Is it not possible to hold that some other cultural idea, of modern India for example, is also the hope of the world? These are curious questions which Kallen's discussion of the "uses" of the American idea will have to consider.

It is perhaps an aspect of the American mind that once Americans feel that they have discovered something good and worth while they want to make it immediately available to all men. Doubtless they are to be admired for this. If the early concepts of Point-Four, the United Nations and even the beginnings of the League of Nations are to be applauded, however, it is also necessary to call up the suspicion and distrust such concepts have caused. Why are there fears that the Point-Four Program will become a military aid project? Why do many Europeans and Asiatics see American culture only as materialistic? Why do they know little or nothing of the ideas that have grown into and developed as a part of the American scene? Is it because the vision of the American idea has at times become obscured by those very forces which Kallen largely ignores? Because Kallen fails to see the unfavorable reoccurrences present in the interplay of repetition of the old with the unique new, which makes culture dynamic rather than static, he will not find an answer.

Faulty though his concept of work, his disregard of historic American forces towards uniformity and his non-recognition of outside sources which have fertilized American culture are, Kallen's view of the American Idea as being the richest fruit so far produced is well worth exploring. Especially is this significant at a time when America leads the world. In the long run it is the ideas of man that have lasted over and above their other works, even though in fact these latter contribute to the very making of the ideas. It is likewise true that ideas have to be re-thought, re-presented and re-defined anew for every generation. This is both helpful and necessary to insure the growth of the best of the American tradition. This is what Kallen attempts to do. His efforts are laudable.

SOME QUERIES FOR

PROFESSOR KALLEN

by *Milton R. Konvitz*

Professor of Industrial Relations, New York
State School of Industrial and Labor Relations, Cornell University

I had always assumed that Horace Kallen's individualism was more radical, more extreme, than that of John Dewey, but now, after reading "Cultural Pluralism and the American Idea," I am not so sure.

Dewey had warned against the separation of "individual" from "social." These terms, he contended, should be used as adjectives rather than as nouns; they should be taken as descriptive of traits of human beings, traits "which are so integral that they are but two aspects of man in his actual existence." He would speak, he said, not of the "individual" but of the "human being." The term "social," he said, "stands for properties which are intrinsic to every human being," and the term "individual" for traits which are "differential, singular, or individual, in the constitution of human beings." He was opposed to "the *separation* of individual and associative [social] aspects of the unitary human being," and to a "personalism" which "ascribes 'independent reality and ultimate value to the individual person alone'!"

Now, Professor Kallen in "Cultural Pluralism and the American Idea" seems to identify himself with proponents of the American Idea whom the "image of the human person signalizes his irreducible individuality." The American Idea which he affirms "starts with the individual." But the image is not that of an absolute. Kallen rejects a "pluralism of absolutes" or "an absolutistic pluralism." He sees a Monad with doors and windows, which sustains its identity "by communication, not by segregation." This is a pluralism which "postulates individuality, particularity, as primal"; yet it does not deprive "the human person of his dynamic relations with his neighbors, . . . On the contrary, it recognizes that the relations do really relate without identifying; . . ." Professor Kallen projects a "relativist pluralism which the living individual encounters in the transactions wherewith he constructs his personal history, moving out of groups and into groups, engaging in open or hidden communion with societies of his fellows, every one different from the others, and all teamed together, . . ."

Are Kallen and Dewey far apart? Kallen would like to think of the individual as in some sense primary, yet this individual has relations that "really relate without identifying," and its identity is sustained "by communication, not by segregation." The individual is not an absolute. Is he, then, essentially different from Dewey's human being whose social traits are intrinsic to him?

I am not offering arguments in a debate. I am asking, respectfully and hopefully, for further elucidation, clarification. The issue is, to my mind, a vital one. Personally—without going into the reasons at this time—I would take a stand in favor of a radical individualism, to which every man is an Adam who is a sub-creator under God; a creature-creator who makes a world for himself; a being few of whose relations do really relate but most of whose relations are quite extrinsic to his reality. I say this not by way of argument with or against Horace Kallen but to provoke further his own thoughts.

AMERICAN INDIVIDUALISM AND

HORACE KALLEN'S IDEA

by Leo Pfeffer

Assistant Director, Commission on Law and Social Action, American
Jewish Congress

I wonder if social philosophers are plagued with the same
timidity and lack of assurance in their own propositions that
impel lawyers to seek out and magnifiy even the most tenuous
similarity to something that may have been said, the longer ago
the better, by other lawyers in the form of judicial decisions.
It is a rare judge who will announce a new legal idea with a
frank admission that it is new, but that it is reasonable and
called for by the new conditions facing the judge. Almost in-
variably the judge will seek to show that the idea really is old
stuff, going back perhaps to the Year Books of Edward I or at
least Blackstone's Commentaries.

Is it the same felt need for a father-authority or is it simply
modesty that requires Professor Kallen to seek to identify cultural diversity with hoary American tradition? For I assume
that he employs the term "American Idea" as the idea of
America, rather than the idea for America. If it is the latter,
I have no quarrel with Professor Kallen. If it is the former,
I suggest that he is unfair to himself and to his monumental
and truly original contribution to democratic social thinking.
The American motto has never been "Liberty, Equality, Diversity." On the contrary, it has long been *E Pluribus Unum*,
with the emphasis on the last word.

Suggestions of the desirability of permanent diversity may
perhaps be found here and there among the main currents of
early American thought. With a little imagination one can
trace the roots of any idea almost anywhere. Professor Kallen,

for example, finds much significance in the fact that the original proposal for a Great Seal of the United States envisaged a shield divided into six quarterings symbolizing the six major lands of origin of the American peoples. (I may suggest that perhaps more significance lies in the fact that this proposal was *not* accepted.) Or one might suggest Roger Williams' famous analogy of the ship that goes to sea with "both papists and Protestants, Jews and Turks" in its hold. Another example might be Madison's argument that "Security for civil rights must be the same as that for religious rights; it consists in the one case in a multiplicity of interests and in the other in a multiplicity of sects." Even here, however, it should be noted, diversity is deemed desirable not for its own sake, not because of any concept of "orchestration," but simply as a means of securing liberty. This was no more an "American" idea than was Voltaire's similar argument that "If there were one religion in England, its despotism would be terrible; if there were only two, they would destroy each other; but there are thirty, and therefore they live in peace and happiness."

Actually, the generation that brought forth the Declaration of Independence and, fifteen years later, the Bill of Rights was concerned with liberty and equality, not diversity. Whatever concern it had with diversity was an incident of its concern with liberty, and if it thought of diversity at all, it thought of diversity of individuals, not of groups or cultures. It is in this respect that any claim that cultural pluralism is just good old traditional Americanism appears to me to be untenable. For culture necessarily implies groups and associations, and cultural pluralism implies cultural groups and associations. It implies, in Professor Kallen's words, "equal liberty, not only for individuals as such but also for their societies and institutions."

But those who inspired the Declaration of Independence and the Bill of Rights were more than suspicious of societies and institutions and associations. Their experience with institutions and associations had not been such as to induce any effort to encourage or secure their preservation. On the contrary, their experience with the religious institutions or associations constituting the several established churches led on the one hand to the pietistic Great Awakening of Jonathan Edwards and George Whitefield and on the other to the enlightenment and skepticism of Paine and Jefferson. Disparate as were the revivalism of the former and the rationalism of the latter, they were united in their hostility to institutional or associational religion and in the conviction, crystallized in the Virginia Statute for Religious Liberty and in the First Amendment to the Constitution, that religion is exclusively a matter between the individual and his Creator or his conscience.

The suspicion of, if not hostility to, religious institutions and associations on the part of the people in the last quarter of the 18th century was duplicated in respect to political institutions and associations. This feeling, bred out of their unhappy experience with the English government, manifested itself in their strong reluctance to accept the new central government proposed by the Philadelphia convention. It manifested itself also in Washington's Farewell Address with its deprecation of political factions.

The great commercial and industrial institutions and associations were still a century away when the Republic was established, but there can be little doubt that these too would have been viewed with less than cordiality or affection. The popular opposition to the progenitor of these, Hamilton's United States Bank, indicates this quite convincingly. And I find no evidence to support any conclusion other than that if the American people of the late 18th century had thought of cultural institutions and associations at all, their feeling toward this would have been suspicious if not antipathetic.

The American Idea when the Republic was founded was liberty, equality and individualism (which is something vastly different from pluralism, religious, political, economic or cultural). And it was this Idea that was secured by the Constitution. The right of association was protected by the Constitution, but what was protected was the right of individuals to associate, not the associations formed by virtue of that right. It was almost a century after our nation was established that the Supreme Court read into the Constitution a guaranty of the rights of corporations, the economic associations spawned by the Industrial Revolution. Up to that time the rights recognized by the Constitution were rights of individuals, and if diversity is a right guaranteed by the Constitution—as undoubtedly it is—it is a right belonging to individuals.

Nevertheless, the Constitution is a remarkable document and the Supreme Court a remarkable institution. It is the power of the Court to interpret the Constitution so as to accommodate its majestic commands to the needs of succeeding generations that has made of the Constitution a living, dynamic instrument and has enabled it to survive and thrive. The revolutionary expansion of American industry demanded judicial protection of economic associations under a Constitution established by an individualistic, agrarian generation, and the Court was able to meet the demand. Similarly, I believe, the survival and expansion of American social democracy demands protection under the Constitution of cultural associations, even though the generation that established the Constitution did not contemplate cultural associations and probably would have viewed them with suspicion if they had.

The Supreme Court seems to have recognized this. A series of decisions over the last three decades has conferred constitutional protection upon cultural pluralism. In one decision the Court invalidated a statute that sought to outlaw parochial and secular private schools and to compel all children to obtain their secular education in state schools. In others it struck down statutes that sought to prevent the operation of foreign language schools and to prohibit the teaching of foreign languages to children. In other decisions it frustrated governmental attempts, through licensing, taxes and denial of bulk-rate mailing privileges, to hamper the publication of newspapers and periodicals whose political or cultural contents were not approved by governmental officials. It held also that a state could not forbid the exhibition of a motion picture deemed sacrilegious by a particular religious faith or of another deemed disturbing to local concepts of the proper relations between whites and Negroes. It refused to permit a state to discriminate, in allowing use of its parks for religious meetings, between conventional and unconventional sects. It held that a state might not require all children in public schools to salute the flag notwithstanding conscientious objectors, and it struck down an attempt by a state to deprive a sect of its assets merely because its spiritual head is a citizen of Soviet Russia.

It is significant that almost all of these decisions were unanimous or nearly so, with but one or at most two justices dissenting in a few. The significance becomes much greater when it is realized how politically variegated was the personnel of the Court during this period, ranging from the ultraconservatism of the Court headed by William Howard Taft and the liberalism of the Roosevelt Court headed by Harlan Stone. These decisions and their near unanimity seem to me to constitute a recognition by the Court that American democracy today demands constitutional protection for cultural pluralism.

The Constitution and the Court can protect cultural pluralism; neither can promote or advance it. That is the task of the people, and the record of the people has hardly been encouraging. Cultural pluralism, as Professor Kallen shows, implies equality, and where conscious efforts have been made to preserve cultural diversity they have generally been characterized by inequality. Organizations, governmental and private, devoted to preserving the culture of the American Indian operate on the patronizing premise that the Indians are wards or children—interesting, lovable and deeply wronged children, but children, nevertheless, who cannot be really expected to protect themselves. The Southern defenders of jim-crow preach separate but equal and the preservation of Southern cultural patterns because they know, of course, that separate means unequal and white supremacy.

Mostly, however, the efforts of the American people have knowingly or unknowingly been exerted toward expunging rather than preserving cultural diversity. It is not without significance that Professor Kallen stresses cooking and dining as aspects of culture, for it is almost there alone that cultural diversity is widely regarded as desirable—witness champagne, pizza, borsht, chow mein, chile con carne, shishkabob, smorgasbord, etc. Elsewhere, the idol is uniformity, sometimes euphemized as unity as in the case of the desperate ecumenical efforts of Protestant church leaders to crowd all non-Romanist denominations under one theological umbrella.

One need only point to the Asian Exclusion Acts, to the national origins quota system in our immigration laws, to the terrifying consequences of political nonconformity, to the ever-increasing mergers of corporations and the resultant standardization of consumers' products, and, by far most threatening, the terrible conformity-producing effects of our major cultural transmitter, the radio, television, cinema and similar mass-communication media. Perhaps ultimate and total conformity will be the end product of a thermonuclear Armageddon; there is nothing more monistic than the rubble of an annihilated civilization.

Nevertheless, the outlook is not all black. The Asian Exclusion Acts have been repealed. The McCarran-Walter Immigration Law, even as it retained the national origins quota system, did provide for at least token immigration from all countries and all cultures. The nadir of political conformity appears to have passed and the voice of the dissenter is again beginning to be heard in the land. Even television can be made as effective a means of preserving cultural diversity as it is of destroying it.

My point is that cultural pluralism, though not, as Professor Kallen seems to suggest an original component of the American Idea, is nevertheless in complete harmony with American constitutional democracy as that has evolved. It is an American ideal rather than an American idea, an ideal or end that, as Professor Kallen observes, we will never achieve but will always be achieving. Despite the odds, it is a struggle well worth waging.

A CRITIQUE OF KALLEN'S CULTURAL PLURALISM

by *Goodwin Watson*

Professor of Education, Teachers College, Columbia University

One who wholly shares Professor Kallen's appreciation of the virtuous cultural pluralism which emerges from the American Dream and the historic struggles of business classes, labor, women and numerous ethnic groups for recognition, freedom and equality, is reluctant to develop minor points of disagreement lest these seem to imply some dissatisfaction with the objective. Quite akin, however, to the ideal of American life as enriched by the diversities it cherishes, is the scientific view that free give and take of honest criticism is a rewarding method of progress for all concerned.

Our first demurrer is not really vital to Professor Kallen's basic thesis. For reasons which he never makes explicit, he devotes a fair portion of his first lecture to the distinction between "culture," as a correlate of leisure (nighttime) and man's productive (daytime) work. The picture of labor, as drawn in these paragraphs, while probably true for most peoples in the past, does not quite fit the current American situation. Automation is replacing the assembly line and the purely repetitive human performance has less and less place in industry. Several opinion surveys indicate that workers today frequently get more "consummatory" satisfaction out of their activities on the job than they do out of their vaunted "leisure." In other words, Professor Kallen has failed to revise the picture of "labor" which intellectuals conceived about the year that Ford put in the assembly line and Charles Chaplin enacted *Modern Times*. That oft-reproduced picture has now become obsolescent and a more accurate account might have served

Professor Kallen's thesis even better. In the anthropological view, as he says, patterns of production are often central to the culture. The classic study by Linton and Kardiner showed how a change from dry rice cultivation (Tanala) to raising rice on flooded land (Betsileo) transformed family life, social relations and even religious observances. When all of culture is seen to have an important relationship to ways of work some interesting questions arise. Are there some relationships between the economic structure of a society and its potentialities for the kind of cultural pluralism Professor Kallen endorses? This would be a promising theme for another book.

The second set of problems arises from some social psychological analysis of Professor Kallen's picture of the educated individual who embodies what Professor Kallen regards as a high and admirable adaptation to cultural diversities. "Actually," he says, "the more 'culture' any of them has acquired, the more liberal or general his education has been, the fuller is his awareness of the values of the Out-groups, the freer are his powers to avail himself of them, and the more abundant his means wherewith to comprehend and enjoy them. His equipment constitutes his cultural mobility; it renders him, mind and body, a cosmopolitan, literally a citizen of the world. Without ever losing his commitment to his home base, his citizenship, and culture, he is now also no stranger in any different country and culture.

"Moreover his mobility between cultures is an extension of his mobility within this cultural home base."

It is the dilettante connotation of culture which makes this picture of the "cosmopolitan" plausible. If we think of culture not superficially in terms of graphic arts, music or literature, but as the firm cradle of custom in which the baby is laid and which inevitably forms his emotional life, his food habits, his language, his thoughts, his skills, his sexual life, his work, and his moral values, the envisioned fluid "cultural mobility" becomes rather incredible. One cannot be brought up in all languages, all family patterns, all religions, and all vocations. What does seem possible, and this may well have been what Professor Kallen had in mind, is that degree of flexibility which comes from attempts to recognize the limiting effects upon oneself of having been formed by one specific culture. One can loosen and broaden this early formation a bit—learn a few more languages—play musical instruments of a different tradition—learn to like some strange foods—try one's hand at several styles of earning a living. But there are, and maybe there should be, some limits to the chameleon qualities of the mature adult. Professor Kallen, for example, would probably be regarded by devout Roman Catholics and ardent Communists as very much a "stranger" to essential aspects of their culture. He "understands" them only as an Out-group critic. Would he argue for the desirability of a more complete identification with their values?

Here is where the Kallen lectures finally fall short of a realistic struggle with the problems of our divided world. One can easily enough "orchestrate" the diverse cultures of mankind if one is free to select only the harmonious instruments and to suppress dissonances. Is there a minimum basis of agreement with our values which we are justified in demanding from others if we are to accept them, to affirm them, to enjoy them, to cherish them? Professor Kallen speaks with admiration of those Northerners who fought the Civil War to win freedom for the slaves. Could not one argue from the premises of his cultural pluralism that those Northerners before, during and after the Civil War failed miserably to achieve a "sporting union of cultural diversities as peers and equals"? Does Professor Kallen's closing sentences seriously propose that we—however enamored of our American Idea—should nevermore engage in "suppression or frustration of any culture, local, occupational, national or international—however totalitarian they may be"?

III

REPRISE:
PLURALISM, CULTURE, FACT, FANTASY, AND FAITH

PLURALISM, CULTURE, FACT, FANTASY, AND FAITH

by Horace M. Kallen

I

The persons, the places, the events and the ideas of our daily lives come and go as singulars. We experience them as individuals. Each occurs, particular and distinct, and gives way to some other not less concrete, in a process of dislocation which is sometimes the same as extinction. Diversity and multitude qualify our concepts and our percepts alike. Regularly, the determination of identity, and our other conceptional operations as well, is an activity of identification. It consists of a bringing and holding together of differents by means of still another different which we employ as a sign or symbol in such wise as to carry the differents on a feeling of sameness that stretches over multitudinous times and spans manifold spaces. We call such ingathering with its suffusion of all by all, whereby the heterogeneous Many are assimilated into a homogeneous One, conception. And we acclaim the result as eternal and universal, always and everywhere the same.

Concept is our word for such results. The concept's role in our vital economy is to translate the strange into the familiar, the unique into the repetitive, the free into the necessary, Tyche into Ananke. We employ concepts to harness up diversification and multitude, to order and drive them according to our need or desire, to impel them upon a gradient of our preference to a goal of our choice. The concept is our postulate of prophecy and prediction. We feel, whenever we have formed one, that we have won to understanding, and we appraise the winning as the success of a somehow independent power, a superior, a supernatural entity, which tradition calls the Reason, the Intellect, the Intelligence. Traditionalists declare that this power reaches behind and beyond the concrete actuals of perception to an insight which renders us one with the One reality, the One value, whereof the actuals are only manifold passing appearances, only diversifiedly perishing tokens. And here, not traditionalists alone, but most of us, are disposed to stop.

Here the process of conceptualizing becomes a sentiment of rationality, a syndrome where familiarity and ease, reassurance and safety, change and certitude, suffuse one another in an ongoing awareness; where the present holds no menace, the future no mystery; where the alien has become intimate and the heartless cordial. In this state of mind we no longer feel impelled to ask *Why? How? What for?* We take understanding as self-evident and ultimate. We appraise it as the cause which has itself for effect, as the Whole which is the identifying substance of all its parts, as the explanation of everything, which yet requires no explanation itself, the Revelation which is no mystery, and requires neither study nor interpretation. Tradition signalizes it with still other synonyms. It translates the psychological sentiment of rationality into the metaphysical intuition of the True, the Good, the Beautiful, the Right.

Perhaps ridiculously, reason is not always and everywhere self-evident, nor understanding self-explanatory. All too unhappily, the sentiment of rationality is a passing sentiment, and the syndrome of familiarity, ease, reassurance and safety is too inwardly involved with the dynamics of aliency, hardship, uncertainty and insecurity. In this context, curiosity craves a reason for rationality; mankind experience a need to understand understanding. The tradition also includes doubters ever searching, seeking, inquiring, never coming enduringly to rest in any finding, on any answer. Their quest takes them round at last to the concrete individualities of perceptual experience; to where conceptions are initiated, and words and other formations of signs and symbols have their beginnings. At these turning points of experience they perceive understanding as perception's stand-in (do not the Germans say, *Ver-stehen* and *Ver-stand?*); they assist at conception's birth in a teamplay of hand and eye, the hand grasping as the eye sees, the eye seeing as the hand grasps; they recognize that one's concept is liter-

ally what one handles together, that is, what one com-pre-
hends; they observe that when one is asked to understand, he is
asked to "see," to "get it," to "get a grip on it," "take it in."
(What here is overt is prehensile and absorptive behavior, denoted by such Latin-derived words as *com-prehend, com-
prendre, capire,* and the Germanic *Begriff* and *Begreifen.*)
They reflect that the Greeks, the first people to have a word
for reason and reasoning, and the first craftsmen of this art, denoted reason by *logos,* that *logos* is their word for word, and
that reasoning or logic is, first and last, a mode of relating
words, and that *the logos* is this mode appraised as transcend-
ent and hypostatized; thus transvalued from a tool into an idol.
Cultural anthropologists tell of magic power attributed to
words, of the fear, the secreting, and the worship of names and
words. Sociologists note the primacy of wordings in the configuration of the cultures, and philosophers and theologians
signalize the word's hypostasis and deification: *"In the beginning was the Word, and the Word was with God, and the
Word was God . . . And the Word was made flesh, and
dwelt among us."* . . .

What may such observations point toward, for those seekers
who find the sentiment of rationality a satisfying transaction
between a person struggling for self-preservation or survival
with a diverse and diversifying circumambience of thoughts,
things and other persons, similarly struggling? And what else
are these struggles for survival or self-preservation known-as,
than a multitude of singular struggles to go on struggling?
This multitude we aggregate and grasp as one; by converging
them we bring them to the conception whose consequence is
understanding. Conception and understanding are the tactics,
the strategy and the logistics of our struggle to go on struggling, each of us an individual different from all the others,
and seeking so to live together with the others that he may
grow the more safely toward his salvation, his freedom, his
happiness.

Even when his understanding is concurrence or agreement,
it must work as a vindication of his own difference. Not his
own but the other fellow's ideas are the obscure ones, the ambiguous, imprecise, never adequately clear and distinct ones,
the ideas always and everywhere in need of clarification and

refinement, of being transcended by different terms in different relations. What in him is self-evident becomes opaque in the other; what in him is infallible certitude becomes guesswork and fallacy in the other.

Conversely, his own signs and symbols, which he has devised in order to reveal his meanings with unfailing precision, are treated by the other as a jargon of ambiguities imposing translation and elucidation. Soon or late, and soon rather than late, every revelation comes to figure as a palimpsest or cryptograph which those to whom it is revealed must needs decipher and translumine for themselves. Soon, rather than late, philosophy and religion, the sciences and the arts figure as aggregations of such palimpsests and cryptographs whose deciphering becomes a mystic art of disclosing a secret which brings salvation to those privileged to receive the disclosure. Scholarship and criticism, it seems to me, up to the current schools of philosophic "analysis" and "value-theory," are enterprises aiming, each according to its kind, to reveal revelation and evince the self-evident by means of still other cryptographs, to the profane more opaque and mysterious than those they purport to decipher, and more necessitous of decipherment themselves. If not, why the endless chain of interpretations of originals, of interpretations of the interpretations, with their challenges, their disputes, their contradictions and transpositions? What else, indeed, makes up the body of criticism and spans the practices of even the most traditionalist schools of theologians, sociologists, literary critics or philosophers?

We confront here a human condition, intrinsic perhaps to every mode of communication between person and person, culture and culture. Awareness of it—I am poignantly aware—is not exemption from it, and I feel nakedly unexempt. Let this excuse me for observing that the differences between the challengers of the views I have here expressed, and the diversities of their challenges compose of themselves an exemplification of these views.

As I read them, the challenges are dual. One group argues errors of fact, by omission or commission. The other group disputes my judgments and appraisals; it argues errors of value.

Since facts are whatever is signified by documents and records, their determination is usually accomplished whenever different inquirers come, for the time being, to a consensus regarding that which the signs signify.

Such consensus appears to be the effective ground of what philosophers, scientists and others intend by "objectivity." In practice it means a process of communication achieved and going on freely without dissent or conflict; it means many minds at once pooling and sharing perceptions or ideas and thence agreeing that the experience which this collective operation eventuates in is experience of an autonomous existence external to and unaffected by the processes which their operation consummates. It is "objective" and opposed to "subjective" as multitude is opposed to singularity or public to private. Perceptions or ideas which one person cannot get others to share or agree to are deprecated as "subjective," regardless of the conviction with which their thinker or perceiver declares their objectivity. And conversely each culture of mankind abounds with beliefs in the objectivity of things and persons and events which men of other cultures assign to collective subjectivity. In the perspectives of the histories, the anthropologies, the other sciences of man and the sciences of nature, "objectivity" and "subjectivity" signify not facts but appraisals. All indicate that perceptions and ideas get transvalued from "objectivity" to "subjectivity" and back again. They are replete with instances of things first "objective" to a single person and "subjective" to the rest of his community which later get revalued to a collective "objectivity" that might become global. They suggest that anything, present, past or future, may figure as "objective" in one culture and be "subjective" to all others.

The qualifications are not intrinsic to percepts or ideas; they are accruals. They are not primarily attributes of *what* a thing is, or of *how* it got that way, but of how it signifies in a personal or an interpersonal history. Our daily lives are everywhere marked by struggles to persuade or force other people to agree that some article of our faith is objective and not subjective, or that some article of their collective faith is subjective and not objective. Our daily lives are everywhere a sequence of transactions in which objectivity stands for subjectivity become collective and public, and subjectivity stands for objectivity private to one or few believers. Scientific method is the current name for the rules of fair dealing which these transactions have generated.

Instead of vindicating a claim to objectivity by trying the believer in an ordeal by imprisonment, by combat, by water, by fire, scientific method establishes objectivity by a trial of his belief. It has, for obvious reasons, generated many synonyms for "belief," such as hypothesis, theory, postulate. It has even used such words as law and principle in this meaning. But all signify a present perception or idea, prophetic of a future event. The issue is the reliability of competing prophecies. It is a bet on the future. And instead of settling the bet by a manhandling or a duel or a battle royal of the bettors, scientific method undertakes to settle it by testing that which they bet on. Its procedure is to assure to different beliefs equal opportunity to match their claims of objectivity freely, safely and justly, without privilege and without penalty. I repeat, "beliefs." For first and last, every assertion and every denial of objectivity is an act of faith presently taking what it says for its own future evidence and its own substantial future. Scientific procedure but undertakes to move the seat of the efficacious evidencing and substantive action as far as possible from the believer's believing to the discursive and operational consequences of that which he believes in. Of course, the seat of its own efficacy is the user's belief in the method and trust in its consequences. But his use of it does displace the war of extinction between believers with a collective insurance by all believers to each that his belief shall have the same chance as its rivals freely and safely to make good his claims for it, and that its performance shall be judged by its consequences, not his superior force. In intention, the American Idea is this method extended to the moral, the political and the cultural economy of the peoples.

Let this be my response to Dr. Flower's very cogent queries on method.

Now I can but hope that I may not fall too far short of this method and intention in reviewing the comments with which my distinguished critics have generously honored this essay of mine. My responses combine their diversities into three major configurations alternative to my own. I read most of them as either restatements or reconciliations of the perennial struggle over the One and the Many, the Absolute and the Relative seen as changing relationships between individual and group, person and institution, labor and leisure in the cultures of mankind, and primarily in the culture of the American people.

II

Milton Konvitz's question touches me closely, since, after William James, John Dewey has been the foremost spokesman for the articles of a philosophic faith most of which we agreed upon and whose intention in works we shared. We shared them to the point of beginning together a statement on the significance of individuality and individualism in the American scene, and soon found such divergence that I completed the statement alone. It was published in 1933 with the title, "Individualism—an American Way of Life." Now I do not feel that my perception of and belief in the primacy of the individual have been replaced by another perception and belief, nor has anything I have subsequently learned, either positively challenged or failed to strengthen the views I then held. It is true that I now tend to say "person" oftener than "individual." But it is more significant of my views that I tend to say "interpersonal," rather than "social." For it seems to me a matter of little importance how "intrinsic" any quality may be to human beings, or how identically it may repeat itself in multitudes of them. The important fact is that the repetitions are many and not one, and that their mere numerical diversity consummates in aggression, hatred and killing at least as often as in more so-called "social" consequences. Identical twins, repeating each other's traits in every cell and every feature, subject to being mistaken for each other by everybody else, still identify themselves as individuals each different from the other, and capable of all the transactions that diversity can initiate. I believe in the primacy of the individual because I can find no other human seat than individuality for choice, for decision, for the initiation of action. I hold it to be the matrix for that "free floating freedom" which Dewey regards as illusory; yet which is postulated for the initiative that is the *sine qua non* for upsetting the inertia of any system, whether intra-atomic or social. "Social action" seems to me analogous to what the physics of today calls "chain-reactions." Where these become repetitive sequences we call them institutions, folkways, mores, customs, laws, manners, morals. The centrifugal tendencies of the individuals who compose the chain of them are, no doubt, less visible than the sequential enchainment. But every individual engenders them even as he undergoes "socialization," "acculturation," "assimilation" and the like. If he succeeds in setting up a chain-reaction he is appraised as a reformer, a revolutionary, a savior, an inventor, a creative genius. If he doesn't, he is appraised a fool, a madman, or a criminal. And given the circumstances, all these terms are used interchangeably.

My endeavor has been not to seek consistency, or to make points in argument, but to keep as close to the actualities of experience as I was able, and I think I have done so. It may be, too, that I have had some influence on Dewey's views. Six years after the publication of "Individualism," in 1939, the great instrumentalist contributed a paper to a collection edited by Clifton Fadiman, in which he wrote: "I should now wish to emphasize more than I formerly did that individuals are the finally decisive factors of the nature and movement of associated life . . . only the voluntary initiative and voluntary co-operation of individuals can produce social institutions that will protect the liberties necessary for achieving genuine individuality." His measure of "social" action became its contribution to the "increase of voluntary, free choice and activity on the part of individuals." That the emphasis may not have turned out to be lasting is another story, not without bearing on the human condition that the seat of value is ineluctably the individual, and that individuals, however intimately they live together with each other, are different from each other even in their likenesses.

Leo Pfeffer's comment seems to me to involve the same issues as Prof. Konvitz's. But his frame of reference is less a philosophic faith and more that of a great libertarian practicing lawyer's perspective of the legal and political changes in American history. Although he does discern, and approve, a trend toward cultural pluralism in the national life, he asserts that it occurs as a contingent variation and not as a natural emergence from the primary intention of the American Idea. He would accept it as the idea *for* America but not as the idea

of America. I hold that Mr. Pfeffer's distinction implies certain misleading assumptions about the relation of ideas and
ideals to events. If one treats them as simply perceptions or
images or conceptualizations of events, whose role is only
somehow to mirror them, the American Idea figures as but an
idea *of* America, and a distorted one. If one treats them as
programs of change, as faiths at work to turn events in new
directions, toward different goals, then the American Idea is
faith making itself into fact. It starts as an idea *for* America,
which consequentially realizes itself in events as the idea *of*
America. It is an achievement of the creative intelligence,
evoked by crisis and employed to vanquish it.

The history of the United States of America, it seems to
me, confirms this way of appraising ideas and ideals: both the
Declaration and the Constitution are articles of faith and plans
of work upon human relations giving them new terms as
theory and as practice.[1] The phrases and images which have

---

[1] The Founding Fathers were convinced of this, I need not repeat. So were
their epigons, each in his own way reaffirming the elders' faith. Did not even
conservative, compromising, fundamentalistic Daniel Webster, the first
American, if I remember correctly, to use the expression, "un-American,"
assert that "with America and in America a new era commences in human
affairs"? Did not absolutist abolitionist, rebelling William Lloyd Garrison
accuse the *de facto* embodiment of Theodore Parker's *de jure* "government
of all the people, by all the people, for all the people" of subverting the
national faith in the "natural law as expressed in the Declaration . . ." that
is, of failing to enact the idea *for* America into the idea *of* America? And
listen to Herman Melville, ten years before the Civil War, in "White-Jacket"
asserting: "In many things we Americans are driven to a rejection of things
of the past, seeing that, ere long, that van of the nations must, of right, belong to ourselves. There are occasions when it is for America to make
precedents, and not to obey them. We should, if possible, prove a teacher
to posterity, instead of being the pupil of bygone generations. More shall
come after us than have gone before; the world is not yet middle-aged . . .
we Americans are the peculiar, chosen people—the Israel of our time—we
bear the ark of the liberties of the world.

"We are the pioneers of the world; the advance guard sent on through the
wilderness of untried things to break a new path in the New World that is
ours. In our youth is our strength; in our inexperience, our wisdom. At a
period when other nations have but lisped, our deep voice is heard afar. Long
enough have we been skeptics with regard to ourselves, and doubted
whether, indeed, the political Messiah had come. But he has come in us, if
we would but give utterance to his promptings. And let us always remember
that with ourselves, almost for the first time in the history of the earth,
national selfishness is unbounded philanthropy; for we cannot do good to
America, but we give alms to the world."

become their symbols signalize their design. It is not unnatural that an American whose paramount vocation is the legal vindication of personal liberty, as is Mr. Pfeffer's, should treat liberty as if limited to this relation, hence, as an isolated concept, self-contained and self-containing, unconnected with diversity and plurality, especially the plurality of groups, whether political, economic, cultural or religious. Yet it seems to me that the record, as psychologists and historians view it, takes account of liberty chiefly in terms of groupings; that it does not deny the actuality of groups—at least not of the States and certainly not of the races, sects and cults within them; and that the emphasis is laid on equal liberty for different individuals not in order to abolish or to nullify the diversity of groupings, but to alter their associative structure; to change from isolationist, authoritarian, hierarchical configurations to intercommunicative, democratic and congregational ones. That the adopted symbolism of the Great Seal was not the proposed symbolism does not mean that the groupings which the proposal symbolized were abolished, or that the liberties of their members, *as such members*, were abolished. The intention was never more than to terminate the traditional practice of privileged groups of taking liberties with the equal liberties of any other group. As I read the nation's history, one aspect of it is the struggle to bring this intention to realization. It seems to me that it did apply to the diverse cultures of mankind and that it is manifest in the cosmopolitan piety of Franklin, Paine, Jefferson, Madison, John Adams. I think that a closer reading of the Founding Fathers might lead Mr. Pfeffer to revise his opinions. Whatever the field of action—state rights, personal liberty, religious freedom, free enterprise, labor relations, education, the phrase *e pluribus unum* with the emphasis on the *unum* can be said to symbolize it. But the *unum* of the American Idea is not the *unum* of the tradition. It signifies not unity but union, and a design of union where groups and individuals, severally and collectively, contract together that all will safeguard equal liberty to each. The intention was held to comprehend all human beings, Negroes as Negroes, and in due course women as women. The accepted symbolism of the Great Seal did not shut out this intention, even though the section of the Declaration of Independence denouncing slavery and the slave trade was excised.[2] And what theme more dominated the nation's heart and mind up to and through the Civil War than Abolitionism? The American Union begins, on the record, as a Union of Unions, and of Unions within Unions, each with its own specific, concrete medium, method, and aim of association. Of course, the elemental term in every such union is, as I have always urged, the individual in his indefeasible singularity. But I know of no instance nor, I believe, does Mr. Pfeffer, of an individual building his personal history solely by himself, from himself, on himself; feeding, so to speak, on nothing but his own flesh and spirit and growing by what he feeds on.

The records tell only of individuals communicating with other individuals, maintaining or forming communions and communities either as free men freely co-operating or under *force majeure*, more or less successfully evaded or resisted. In the history of some peoples, the impact of superior power, governing without the consent of the governed, may so affect their sentiments and values as to keep generations of them appraising both the idea of equal liberty and of the patterns of government whose authentic matrix it is, as authoritarian *force majeure*.

A current instance of this consequence may be observed in certain societies of Jews who, celebrating the 300th anniversary of the arrival of a group of their forebears in North America, accepted for the theme of their celebration, "Man's opportunities and responsibilities under freedom." The unique, unprecedented phrase, "under freedom" seems to me a pro-

[2] "He (George III as head of the government of Great Britain) has waged cruel war against human nature itself, violating its most sacred rights of life and liberty in the persons of a distant people who never offended him, captivating them and carrying them into slavery in another hemisphere, or to incur miserable death in their transportation thither. This piratical warfare, the opprobrium of *infidel* powers, is the warfare of the *Christian* King of Great Britain. Determined to keep open a market where *MEN* should be bought and sold, he has prostituted his negative for suppressing every legislative attempt to prohibit or restrain this execrable commerce; and that this assemblage of honors might want no fact of distinguished die, he is now exciting those very people to rise in arms among us, and to purchase that liberty of which he deprived them, by murdering the people upon whom *he* obtruded them; thus paying off former crimes committed against the *liberties* of one people, with crimes which he urges them to commit against the *lives* of another."

jection of the centuries during which the Jewries of Christian
and Mohammedan lands survived only by permission, on suf-
ferance and not as of right, and under penalties imposed *on*
them, simply for being Jews, by the authority of preponderant
powers which governed them without their consent. To most
of mankind freedom is inward, a primal, intrinsic and unalienable right. Permission can only recognize it, not create it. This
mid-century Jewish phrase signalizes it, on the contrary, as a
permissive power, operating, regulating, controlling from
without. "Under freedom" does not occur in the languages
of mankind. Immemorial usage, also in Hebrew, says "in freedom." Freedom is native and original, not alien in human
nature, is that part of the authentic human condition evinced
by the fact that men and women everywhere unite, separate
and work and fight to get out from under.

And in this, all that free men can diversely mean by liberty,
individuality, plurality and equality is dynamically implied.
The words name divergent floods from a single spring of
psychosomatic activity, and wherever one signifies the others
must. This is why, in the perspectives of the American Idea,
the meaning of equality moves from the practices of the am-
bitious whose ideal is "to keep up with the Joneses," render
themselves the same as their "betters," to the conduct of the
self-respecting whose ideal is to make themselves in their
singularity as good as their betters, and better, to affirm the
equality of the unlike, and to exercise the right to be different.
What, besides, can freedom denote except choices and
chances, new directions, new goals, and new forms of association and their concert in speech and action? The last, often
signalized as "government"—literally procedures of steering
and guiding—may begin as a collective means "to secure these
rights"; that is, to secure the distributive ends of Roger Williams' "Papists, Protestants, Jews, and Turks" and of the
countless other organizations of interest taking passage in the
Ship of State which they have built to be the common carrier
to their communally singular destinations.

But the significance of this collective means, like the significance of every other means where the dynamic is a relation
between person and person, lies in whether it actually secures
and nourishes and strengthens the ends for which it was insti-

tuted, or frustrates or abolishes them, and generates or imposes other ends. For in human relations, ends are not external to means and cannot justify them. In human relations, means have the same import for ends as a person's past has for his present. This is why political societies which pretend to prepare people for liberty by means of tyranny, or for democracy by means of dictatorship (whether of the *soi-disant* proletariat, vicar of God, or philosopher-king) are either deceiving themselves or degrading the people from ends-in-themselves into means for alien ends. And this is why Cultural Pluralism, while not identical with "good old traditional Americanism," has to be a growth of that original seed, and is actually one of its truest exfoliations.

III

I may now, in the light of the foregoing, take together the questions raised concerning the *what* of culture in terms of the relations of the labors of day life to the leisure of night life, and the interactions with them of ethnic, religious and other such social heritages.

I find it simplest to begin with the questions raised in Dr. Flower's acute and generous commentary—perhaps because I am not quite sure whether to take it as supplementation or as exception to my views. My disposition is to take it all for supplement and reënforcement; I am quite ready to agree with her defense of the philosophic disciplines, including those contemporary deviations, "analysis" and "value-theory," as vocations worthy of the total commitment of free minds. I am disposed to appraise them as heroic endeavors after a precision denied by their own history and by the nature of things. They are, like all their kind, sisyphean labors, which to me, at least, signalize a definitive trait of *genus humanum*. What I deprecate in them is a certain self-isolation, a cultivated tangency and irrelevancy to the rest of the human enterprise.

The syndrome, I think, is exemplified by the event that protagonists of analysis such as Russell or Whitehead, do not carry its media and methods over into their discussion of the troubles unto which man is born, as the sparks fly upward. In their treatment of paramount issues of culture such as the pursuit of happiness, labor and leisure, war and peace, education, death and immortality, their philosophizing is what Whitehead calls philosophy in *Process and Reality*—"imaginative penetration" quite other than "pinning down the thought to the strict systematization of detailed . . . antecedent observation." Systematization is good, of course, excellent as a servant, but an enslaving and tyrannical master: First and last, logical form, implicative coherence, are tools of procedure, not perceptions of process: as Einstein wrote, "physical concepts are free creations of the human mind, and are not, however it may seem, uniquely determined by the external world." And Whitehead argued in *Adventures of Ideas* that conscious discrimination is itself "a variable factor only present in the more elaborate examples of occasions of experience." In his Ingersoll lecture on Immortality, given in 1940, he declared that "exactness is a fake."

There is good reason to believe that during his years at Harvard, logician Whitehead had come to share certain views of logic with William James, to whom his official biographer ascribed "an almost morbid alogism." Certainly Whitehead also came to perceive that process outruns the exactitude we crave in our struggle to harness the former up and make it go our way. Certainly science, kept solely to tasks of definition and fixation, becomes dogmatism, and as science suicidal, since it stops with a product and replaces production with reproduction. For the inwardness of science is also process, not product; also consequentiality, not finality. But in their craving for ultimates, for invariancies, men of science, like men of religion, are disposed to attach themselves to the latest product as the last, to transvalue working hypotheses into dogmatic laws always and everywhere the same. This converts Nature, the everlasting sequence of diversification into Nature, the eternal and universal system of clear and distinct self-repeating parts, so related to one another as to compose an undivided and indivisible whole. Some scientists, like Messrs. Jeans or Eddington or Compton or Millikan, qualify the whole with one form or another of consciousness, gracing the unhuman theme with the humanizing note for the comfort and salvation of mankind.

Thinking about these matters has brought me, in recent years, to replace the qualification "scientific" for the humanism of my faith with some other word—perhaps "free." The ex-

pression "free humanism" does come closer to the enduring
aspects of my philosophic outlook.

This may suggest why I cannot warm to the notion that
culture is subject to "permissible predicates." One asks immediately, permissible *by* whom, *to* whom? The expression
raises questions of orthodoxy and heresy, of approved usage
and disapproved. It implies fixities which those who perceive
culture as process take to be either reciprocal arrests of movements or static illusions. Orthodox notions are usually authoritarian. They project totalitarian pretensions and programs of
cultural imperialism such as *kultur* has often connoted in international discourse. They permit some predicates and prohibit others. The predicates may signify spontaneous variations
within a culture, authentic native originations with no parallel
anywhere or formations already existing or infiltrating from
other cultures. Often, where orthodox programs fail to realize
the pretensions they are predicated on, their aficionados
compensate the failure by transvaluing its actualities as "appearance," its desiderata as "reality" and proclaiming the
overlordship of this "reality" regardless of all experiences of
its operational impotence. Notions such as "white supremacy,"
"dialectical materialism," "machtmensch," "kunstmensch" I
esteem as of this order, and hence signified by "emotionally
charged slogans." I observe that the compensations which
compose the order are functions of "disconfirming evidence,"
and that their emotional charge seems directly proportional to
their incompetencies as works and ways of changing the
actual.

On the record, we may count as "permissible predicates" of
culture, first, any that a student of culture permits himself; and
again, whatever he is able to persuade others—students and
non-students—to consent to. "Permissible" and "prohibited"
name relationships which an ongoing interchange of signs,
images and ideas elicits or suppresses, impatterns in logical formations and consummates in perceived consequences. The
processes signified by "cultural diffusion" get translated into
an articulate system whenever consents orchestrate alternatives into consensus, and combined dissents segregate individuals into majorities and minorities.

With consensus comes co-operation—and vice versa. Dissent

goes with innovation, invention, and discovery—and vice versa. To attain either or both, the seminal prerequisite is mobility of persons and peoples within and between configurations of culture. Native craftsmen, priests and poets, native philosophers, scholars and missionaries of religion, native peddlers, merchants and fighters, wandering from one home region to another; alien ones wandering freely or being driven from culture to strange culture have, throughout recorded time, been the principals in diversifying the faiths, the works, the functions and the forms predicable of cultures. Such, perhaps more dramatically, have also been wandering cultural communities, of which those that modern man's schooling keeps more visible in his collective heritage are the Greeks, the Hebrews and the Romans.

But Isocrates' observation concerning Hellenic culture holds for all cultures. The sense of this relationship seems to me to be prompting the present theory and practice of diffusion and their current modification in the light of experience with Point Four or its equivalent in Asia and the Americas. This experience seems to confirm certain interpretations of the available data *re* intercultural communication—namely that the brainwashing method does not annihilate, but only represses that which it would wash out; that when the washing stops, the washed soon or late suffuses and gives a new turn to whatever has been superimposed. The record of Latin-American cultures, of the religious cultures of Christian and Moslem Europe and of the Negro and Indian cultures of North America tell the tale, which the errors of method in the administration of Point Four confirm.

Hence the new attitude toward American Indian communities whose chief voice is the Association on American Indian Affairs. Hence the ideal of "the New Negro" whose first prophet was Alain Locke. One recalls Booker Washington's observation in *Up from Slavery:* "We must acknowledge that notwithstanding the cruelty and moral wrong of slavery, the ten million Negroes inhabiting this country, who themselves or their ancestors went through the school of American slavery, are in a stronger and more hopeful condition, intellectually, morally, and religiously, than is true of an equal number of black people in any other portion of the world." Inquire into the fundamental dynamic of such strength, and you uncover the free synergy of heritage and habit. Alain Locke's programmatic ideal of "the New Negro" became the releasing symbol of that confluence. My own word for the process is *orchestration*. It arises unconsciously, spontaneously. Awareness translates it into plan. The tales of Uncle Remus are samples of spontaneous orchestration; the ideal of the New Negro, of orchestration consciously purposed. Purposed orchestration is more likely to succeed where all concerned participate in deciding on its ends and means.

In the United States, the role of the Negro in the cultural process is a highly visible example of the role of every group. "We have wanted a land," Mr. Justice Douglas writes in his dissent in Dennis vs. United States (341 U.S. 494 at p. 585), "where our people can be exposed to all the diverse creeds and cultures of the world." [3] But Dr. Flower asks, Is not this intention ambiguous? Is its interpretation in terms of cultural pluralism alone not likely to be an arbitrary abstraction from the concrete totality which misrepresents the latter? What precisely is an American?

When I try to meet the requirement signified by "precisely," I find myself endeavoring to produce something that will satisfy the questioner, regardless of whether I dissatisfy myself. Multiply the questioners, include the answerer, and your ideal of precision becomes that which will satisfy everybody everywhere and always. So far as I can see no concept, no so-called universal can do this. Every definition hit upon would be drawn from some perceptual particular and handled as the measure of sameness in other particulars. Primarily, an American is anybody who identifies himself as an American. He stays one so long as he goes unchallenged by others, or survives challenge whether from soi-disant Americans or from non-Americans, or he does not himself abandon the identification. On this level he is an American by virtue of an external relation to a configuration of peoples, land and institutions. His identity as American is here one he may have passively acquiesced in, as do most natives; freely chosen, as do all of the naturalized Americans; or actively affirmed and advanced as well. Legally, natives identify themselves as Americans by

[3] I am indebted to Leo Pfeffer for calling my attention to this dissent.

claiming and receiving the protection of their rights at home and abroad from the American government; the foreign-born do so by a public rite at which they freely forswear all allegiance to other governments and swear all allegiance to the Constitution and Government of the United States. A term of this allegiance is that both natives and naturalized are free to change it, without fear and without favor, for a different allegiance. Situations may arise, too, when loyalty to the American Idea may move agents of the American government to persuade Americans by naturalization to change their political allegiance for the sake of the spiritual Americanism of the American Idea. Reluctant Max Brauer's piety to democracy as motive in his finally taking on the arduous responsibilities of first mayor of post-war Hamburg is an instance.

But persons may also identify themselves as Americans or be so identified by others in a different dimension of living. This dimension is internal to their attitudes, works and ways as persons; it is the life line of their personal histories, and consists of the experiences which, beginning as perceptions and surviving as memories, compenetrate into the stuff of character and the dynamic of every person's existence and values, his faith and works. It is in this sense that Max Brauer and George Santayana, for example, became lastingly American even though one returned to German citizenship and the other remained his whole life long a Spanish subject with a Spanish passport. Such inward Americanization occurs whenever any person comes to feel more at home among others calling themselves Americans than among non-Americans. The feeling grows as a process of free communication, both competitive and co-operative, with those others; a process of selecting, appropriating, and assimilating ideas, images, symbols and attitudes, and of participating in events which those signalize as "American." A person's existence as "American" is thus a sequence of transactions, of isolating, pooling, and sharing perceptions, of digesting and compenetrating them into sentiments and attitudes and remembrances whose confluence with those of other "Americans" near and far, at home and abroad, joins him to them in a specific configuration of intimacy.

This has degrees, of course, and I know of no precise measure for its intensities or range. Brauer and Santayana exemplify extremes. The American multitude remain at home. Of each, the sentiment of familiarity, of belongingness, of intimacy, attaches to the continental diversification of lands or waters, of heights, or depths, or flatnesses, of the quiet village, the bustling suburb or the roaring city, and of those who struggle to go on struggling in these varied places through the changing times and seasons. However brief its stretch, the sentiment is a sense of history making itself, a feeling of how past and present mingle their lights to breed the future formations wherewith the many keep themselves, one and all, ongoingly American, and nourish the first person singular who is each American. "The Republic," as Archibald Macleish wrote somewhere, "is a symbol of union because it is also a symbol of differences, and it will endure not because its deserts and seacoasts and forests and bayous and dead volcanoes are of one mind, but because they are of several minds and are nevertheless together. . . . It is where the sand and the marsh and the rock and the grass and the great trees and the eternal wind compose the frontiers of diversity that there is greatness."

Do such sentiments express "uncritical acceptance of diversity for its own sake"? Are they not rather the consequence of a critical study of the relationships which diversities seek with one another, of an appraisal of the nature and consequences of diverse modes of union, of the recognition that diversity is primal and indefeasible, and of the choice of one pattern of their togetherness more reassuring of the equal liberty that the diverse seek?

So then, that which keeps bringing diversity to union, and nourishing the union, is, as I see it, the attitude, the sentiment, which the American Idea, and the more fleshly inference from it, "the American Dream" signalizes. This seems to me the enduring, and hence the least visible factor of the linkage of the diverse peoples and places which qualifies them each and all as "American." And this, of course, is what persons of another culture, with its own qualifying postulates and prejudices, are least likely to perceive. Their appraisals of Americans are, first, a shaping of perception by their own distinguishing postulates and prejudices—*vide* observers from Charles Dickens to André Siegfried and other fascists or neo-fascists, or to Russian Communists and their western comrades. Include even de Tocqueville and Bryce and Brogan and Toynbee. Of course they all select from the multitudinous aggregations that shape themselves around the poles of the American Idea, such highly visible items as confirm those postulates and prejudices of theirs. Of course most of our contemporaries abroad will deprecate such presentations of Americanism as Henry Commager's and see the American as solely a materialist, a rotarian, a dixiecrat, a goon, "Uncle Sham" *und so weiter;* not many will see him as a neighbor in a community of communities all different, and all willy-nilly molding their struggles to live and to grow in accord with the code which is the American Idea. The code articulates the attitude. As compared with both the persons and principles that extend it and those that oppose it its visibility is lower than the record justifies. We take it for granted as we take for granted our bodies and other gradients in the formation of the patterns of togetherness whereof human cultures are variants. Until the movement it channels is barred or deflected, it is no news. News attends the change, the trouble, the exigency, the challenge. It is when some deeply disturbing alteration in the condition of Americans lifts the American Idea from the level of unconscious attitude and routinal creed back again to the level of conscious purpose and fighting and working faith, that it figures as news. Wars have been the most conspicuous occasions of these repristinations. But crises in the economy, natural catastrophes, summations of social injustice, have served as well. The present "age of anxiety," "atomic age," age of "cold war" and "international tensions," is again such a time.

True, as Roscoe Pound has also noted, we do not count one American Dream, nor one American way. It has been my steady contention that we count many. But the many render themselves at one as American only in so far as they agree to hold to the American Idea for the way that all can together keep the peace and assure to one another equal liberty and equal safety for their diversities. Americans may interpret such assurance as did Thomas Jefferson and James Madison and other Founding Fathers, as did Walt Whitman and James Russell Lowell and Henry James, or Mark Twain and Sinclair Lewis. Or they may interpret it as do the Daughters of the

American Revolution, the American Legion, Walter Lipp-
mann, the justices of the Supreme Court or the Fund for the
Republic. But the interpretations of those who are faithfully
committed to it will soon or late be so shaped to one another
that their togetherness will exemplify its affirmation of the
parity of the different in rights to life, liberty and the pursuit
of happiness and their equal partnership in the common undertaking to secure those rights whereof the evidence and substance is government of all the people, by all the people, for
all the people. The undertaking is not the argument of a foregone conclusion. It is not a bet on a sure thing. It is an act of
faith whose hazards it must overcome by its own works. Its
validation is self-validation. It is making good its promise in
achievement.

I do not see how the individualizing trait of the authentic
American can be anything else than his commitment to this
common undertaking of his plural society. His other differentiae as American follow from this. It seems to me, moreover,
that all organizations of interest whatsoever stay authentically
American only as they thus follow the American way laid out
by the American Idea. So doing, they figure as collaborators
in a covenant of toleration toward every interest which is not
itself intolerant, which does not enter the partnership holding
that it is endowed with the right, and motivated by the intention, under the aegis of the covenant, to replace the equal
liberty which it shares with the different by the subjection of
the different to its own power and authority. The American
record seems to be, certainly since the First World War, that
parties to such a covenant of toleration tend to pass, not too
readily, not without travail of blood and sorrow, but to pass,
from the attitude of live-and-let-live to the attitude of live-
and-help-live. However unspontaneous, the passage is a forecast from that prime intention. The latter, once shaped by
means of symbols and creeds into a conscious ideal, becomes
the psyche of that soma, the spirit of that communion of communities which is the nation. It is reverenced as an independent
moral and intellectual system, the articles of a faith which
directs the works wherewith a people expresses its faith in
fact. Faith and works carry on as functions of one another;
they orchestrate into a homeostatic progression of widening

range and scope which some qualify as culture at one of its turns, and as vocation at the other.

IV

I advert now to the issues raised from my description of the relationships between labor and leisure, consumption and production in our cultural tradition and of its bearing on certain persistent appraisals of vocation and culture. My good friend Dr. Goodwin Watson contends, if I understand him, that the matrix of a culture must be economic, and that its development must be a pattern of customs which shapes the life and thought of every individual from birth, so that by implication he is an effect of those causes and only that. "One cannot be brought up in all languages, all family patterns, all religions, all vocations"; one can make oneself flexible, but must not become a cultural chameleon. In relation to Communists and Roman Catholics I stand only "as an outgroup critic."

In reply, I may point out that I have never said one can. I have never minimized the role of economy in a culture, or ignored its role in the folkways and mores of a people. I do however take individuals to be causes as much if not as visibly, as effects, and to be alone the dynamic makers and carriers of the values, the works and the ways whose transmissal we call custom. It is from the differences between individuals that differentiations of custom keep arising, however minutely, and compounding into visible changes. Differences, as I have often repeated, may express themselves in a war of all against all, each fighting to kill or enslave and to reshape the others into means for its own ends. Again, differences may impattern themselves in endeavors toward an orchestration of all with all. The former gets projected in such philosophies as Thomas Hobbes', or the totalitarian pretensions of sacerdotal, racist or proletarian dictatorships. The latter gets projected in such social philosophies as Thomas Jefferson's and the democratic endeavors of pluralistic libertarian societies such as the United States, Great Britain, the Scandinavian countries. The ultimate issue between North and South, between democrats and totalitarians, whether religious or political or economic, is never *what* they are, but how they propose to live together with others—whether as privileged masters or equal associates.

I do not have to become a Communist or a Roman or other Catholic in order to perceive, understand, enjoy and also commit myself to their equal liberty and safety. Although I am very far from being one or the other, I nevertheless can and do orchestrate with both, in so far as they permit me to do so *freely*. Likewise, I am neither a composer nor a musician, but I can and do perceive, understand, enjoy, and believe in many forms of musical expression. The production of that music is the composer's vocation; its performance is the soloist's, the orchestra's vocation; its consumption is my, and every music-lover's, culture. In the same way, the production of the Communist or the Roman Catholic economy or creed and code is their vocation. When I consume their products, those enter my culture, but in a different relation than to their producers'. But when those producers undertake to force their products on me, to compel me to consume them and to support and participate in their production, when they pursue totalitarian ends by authoritarian means, they are using their products to wage war against my freedom. As a party or cult within the In-group they then make a Fifth Column conspiring to betray the libertarian culture of their fellow-citizens to a totalitarian Out-group. As an Out-group, it may be their fighting faith that there is no room among mankind for both their own culture and any other, and that war to the death between the two is a foregone conclusion. Then, until they feel able to bring war to this point, they practice those tactics of force and fraud which are currently known as "cold war." Nothing that I have ever said or written can suggest a policy of nonresistance to such aggression. On the contrary.

Short of these intercultural relationships, however, there are all the others which the American Idea as signifying the democratic process enables. These have for their terms the individuality of individuals and of the groups which are their interpersonal configurations. They recognize how widely and variously these configurations are sustained by an ongoing division of labor whereby every individual is enabled to reach beyond the cultural boundaries set by his vocation, at which he earns his living, to the cultural objects and activities in which he lives his life.

These objects and activities are what his earnings buy for him to consume. They are the products which it is the vocation of other individuals to produce. Consuming them does not render him their producer. But they nourish the insights and skills of his own vocation and serve as a strengthening link between him and their producers. Whether as food of the body or the mind, they bespeak other lives, other labors and other cultures; they are the substances of that diversified vicarious experience by which we are able to reach toward the actual experience of all the world's otherness; they are the symbols and surrogates of that otherness; the vision of it which letters, the sciences and the arts provide us with, whatever we are, wherever we are.

Tradition's over-all distinction between labor and leisure is in no way diminished because some vocations do provide, and because it would be better if all could and did provide, ongoing consummatory experience; if the wage-earner's comminuted productive labor were to hold for him the satisfyingness which their undivided "creative work" is said to hold for artist and scholar. Nor would the divergence be lessened between people's interests and activities when earning their livings and when living their lives. The automations and other "labor-saving" devices of the advancing industrial economy work together with trade-union policy in heightening the over-all distinction. Programs of "adult education," "do-it-yourself" projects, heighten it. Basically they distinguish between work which is a means to other ends than itself, and work which, with play, sport, the "fine" arts and "pure" science, is performed for its own sake, as its own end. There are some occupations in which the earning of a living and the living of a life overlap. But in none can they coincide, for unless consumption has a wider and more diversified range than production, men live like cattle on the range, spending all their waking lives on cropping the fodder which restores the energy they use up in cropping and chewing and digesting the fodder. And this is why culture goes with consumption and is comprehensive, and vocation goes with production and is limited.

What I have said to Goodwin Watson applies as well, I think, and obviously to Mr. Herold Hunt's animadversions. But there are several opacities which justify further comment.

I regret that my exposition of the interdependence as well as of the differences between culture and vocation is not as clear to Mr. Hunt as it is to others. All I had done in fact was to summarize certain social, religious and philosophic traditions wherein the two diversely figure, and to call attention to the configuration their diversity receives from our industrial economy and from the labor movement. I find Mr. Hunt's equation of Renaissance individualist self-realization with work, such as farmers and craftsmen continue to do for gain, one which no reader of Shakespeare, or Spenser, or Castiglione, or Peacham, or Ben Jonson or Molière (to mention only a few Renaissance writers) could accept. Nor can economists or theologians concede without argument that work which is a painful means is qualitatively the same as work which is a satisfying end in itself. The latter, I repeat, is usually equated to sport and play and art; it is related to work as currently amateur golf is to the presidency.

Yes, a theory is of record that certain Calvinists among the Puritans, agonized because they could not know whether Divine Providence had predestined them to eternal life or eternal death, worked that they might make a profit, not to spend on living, but to invest in more work for more profit, until they died. It is held that they practiced a secular asceticism, and hoped that thrift on earth might lay up for them treasure in heaven as well. This is now disputed, but I think there is still a consensus that they valued work in this life as an anodyne for the soul agonized over its own future when dead. Even so they distinguished between servile and the gentlemanly labor, so often indiscernible from leisure-time activities. Perhaps the latter was "the right use of leisure" Mr. Hunt aspires to. On the other hand, here is Bertrand Russell, praising idleness, and distinguishing two kinds of work: the first, "altering the position of matter at or near the earth's surface relatively to other such matter," and "unpleasant and ill paid"; the second, "commanding others to perform these alterations," and pleasant and highly paid. The first is praised, but it is the second that is sought, as conspicuously among Mr. Hunt's Puritans as anywhere. Russell opines that "the morality of work is the morality of slaves and the modern world has no need of slavery."

Now, unless I greatly misread the record, this morality is among the other aspects of Puritanism that the American Idea turns away from. In point of fact, the frontier, not Puritanism, made it recessive, and by the time Benjamin Franklin was declaring that in this country a man is asked not who he is, but what he can do, the Puritanism bespoken by Cotton Mather, John Cotton, Jonathan Edwards, was on its way out, the Enlightenment had arrived, and the Genteel Tradition was in embryo. This is the change I was signalizing when I discussed the rationale of "to make good" as an idiom of American speech.

The rationale seems to me intrinsically American. It illumines the change in the status of democracy from a theory and practice of government generally deprecated and condemned to one approved, and championed with life, fortune and sacred honor. The Declaration of Independence, which articulates it, signalized a new birth of freedom and gave it a local habitation and a name, by Theodore Parker's christening, "The American Idea"—a creedal expression of the ongoing global democratic revolution. Discussing this birth, I had no more call to mention Locke, or Balmaqui, or Plato, or Liliburn or the Levellers or Magna Charta than Mr. Hunt would have to produce a genealogical tree when a child is born. The object of vital concern is the living baby in its singularity, not the dead ancestors. And since my theme has been the relation between Cultural Pluralism and the American Idea, I have not felt called upon to say anything more specific about its diffusion and transvaluation in other lands among other peoples, with their other faiths, other works and other cultural formations. It seemed enough to point to certain dynamic resemblances between the Universal Declaration of Human Rights and the Declaration of Independence, and to show how both are confessions of faith. I have repeated many times that American history is the record of the struggle among Americans to embody this faith in fact. Far from ignoring the opposition in the struggle, I have pointed it up, again and again. Anybody aware of its history can detail the sequences of the struggle, several of which I have specifically referred to, including those for women's rights and against Ku Klux Klanism and other such *isms*.

As for alternatives to the American Idea that the world takes or might take for its hope—there have been many, there are many, there will be many more. Which, depends on what the peoples of the world hope for. Whoever hopes that the Universal Declaration of Human Rights may become a covenant, resting on the common consent of mankind, instituting its articles as the law governing interpersonal, intercultural and international relations, is placing his hope in an extension and elaboration of the American Idea.

On this, it seems to me, and on the philosophy of Cultural Pluralism as a whole, I have an implied confirmation from Dr. Frank Graham, drawing for his comment upon the orchestrated experience of his diverse careers as president of a great Southern state university, United States Senator, member of a commission of the United Nations Organization charged with the problems of freedom and safety of a newly sovereign and independent Asiatic State, and elder statesman of the American people. His dissents are, of course, more evident.

v

Let me turn now to Professor Stanley Chapman's comments. To me they convey a realistic perception of how the American Idea works in certain areas of the soil of which it is a growth; they extend the base of my observations and strengthen my philosophic faith. However, Professor Chapman's findings have led him to use certain expressions which I have myself preferred to replace with others because of the connotations and feelings that usually go with them. I pick out two, "melting pot" and "ghetto." Professor Chapman appears to employ these in antithetic senses. "Ghetto," if I understand him, signifies a little and belittled Out-group, shut off and denied by the larger and superior In-group all friendly contact or communication as equals. Or it signifies a small, self-isolating and isolated, strongly coherent community of people believing themselves to be of the same derivation, of the same vernacular, culture, and the same religious, familial and dietary ways, refusing all avoidable contact with Out-groups except on equal terms and fighting a cold war for that equality. Or its members may appraise the Out-group as superior, take its representatives for the Joneses they want to keep up with, and paying them the compliment of imitation and emulation, deprecate and disvalue the excellences of their Ghetto. The dynamics of the changing relations here involved are anything but those of a melting pot. Many of the elements refuse to melt, others melt too readily for strength, others tend to overspread and mask without fusing, the other metals in the pot. In so far as our country does produce "a new people and a new way of life," it does so, not on the analogy of a melting pot, but of a team of players and workers, or an orchestra. Psychologically, the important quality of this process of innovation is that the past continues alive and free in the ongoing present and contributes a predictable portion of the unpredictable future. This does not occur where ghettos stay isolated. It occurs where they open all avenues of communication, becoming a communion of communities. They thus reciprocally strengthen and enrich their diverse collective individualities and shape themselves into a federal union which grows in and through their free communication. This, I believe, is how our people actually make themselves into "a new people with a new way of life."

Professor Chapman argues that most ghettos are bound to melt away in the pot of changes and chances which is the American political economy, with its designless industrial cities, its abundance of standardized ephemeral consumer goods and services, its profit-taking cult of "consumerism", and the "off-the-job culture" which the cultists cultivate. The latter is a rival to the "heritage cultures" of the American peoples. Those consist in perduring forms of speech, dress and diet, work and play, traditions of song and story, intimately projecting group and personal histories, mores of family, village and town and deeply bound to rotes and rites of church and of creed, all brought from this or that "old country." With the consequence, as Mark Twain half a century ago observed, in his dialogue, *What Is Man?* (Chapter IV), "If you know a man's nationality, you can come within a split hair of guessing the complexion of his religion: English—Protestant; American—ditto; Spaniard, Frenchman, Irishman, Italian, South American—Roman Catholic; Russian—Greek Catholic, and so on. And if you know a man's religious complexion you know what sort of religious books he reads when he wants some more light, and what sort of books he avoids, lest by accident he gets more light than he wants."

Now, fifty years later, these particular hyphens look far less stationary, far more transitive. Today, "American" may signalize a union of Irishman, Italian, South American with Protestant or Judaist: or Russian, or Anglo-Saxon or Jew with Roman Catholic or Protestant, and so on; it may connote "community churches" and interfaith services, it may denote such a qualification of the function of army chaplains, that the clergy of all cults must be able to minister to the needs of every soldier in terms of the rites and rotes of the soldier's own. Here, again, the hyphen signifies relatively durable terms joined together by mobile relations.

Professor Chapman suggests that the process is subject to limitations. Professional "minority mongers" who make a career of exploiting the hyphen, endeavor to hold minorities in the ghetto role, to keep them closed societies, organizations of interest that "expect and demand privileges the majority do not enjoy." Diverse religious societies discourage, many forbid exogamous marriages; they demand, when such do occur, that their children shall be brought up in the doctrine and discipline of the society; some claim eminent domain over any child, orphaned or adopted, and exercise authority over its disposal, without regard to the desires of its parents and the actual good of the child. Every such society employs some technique of appropriation and segregation, in order to hold the young within the fold and shape them body and mind to their own ways and works.

The synergy of such religious isolationism with ethnic cultural heritages, one gathers from Dr. Chapman, is bringing into stable configuration a "fourfold ethnoid group pattern of American communities." He holds, I take it, that religion and color are the actual as well as the traditional potencies of isolation and of ghetto persistence. He foresees the American people distinguishing themselves generally as Protestants, Roman Catholics, Judaists and Negroes. He anticipates an ethnic hierarchy among the Roman Catholics with the Irish the apex. He foresees Protestant denominations moving from the union of their diversities which is the National Council of Churches to a completer digestion of the diversities, perhaps in an univocal conception of faith and works. (He might, to strengthen his prophecy, also have remarked that today's *National* Council began its career as the Federal Council.) He has less to forecast about Judaists and Negroes, about their diversities of interest and organization and the many conflicts within their changing aggregated totalities.

Indeed, I have the impression that Professor Chapman underestimates two things. *First,* how alterative are the transactions between individuals and groups of individuals when the past which they are shapes their perception of the environment they are in; and *Second,* how novel can be the turns and formations which the transactions initiate. He seems to me to lay inadequate stress on individual variations within a culture, and on their capacity for setting off chain-reactions that can break or reshape the configurations they arise in, as neutrons break or reshape molecules and atoms.

The stability of Dr. Chapman's "ethnoid group patterns" seems to me to be continually subject to battering from competing organizations of interest, and to depend for its continuity on how far the members who are its life feel that it assures them freedom, fellowship and fulfillment. Unless "ethnoid group patterns" can make good their claims of actually doing this job better than their competitors, they may become as recessive as the magician medicine man before the scientific medical man, fading from the individual's vital center of value to its periphery, ceasing to figure as necessities and becoming luxuries, intermittently recovering importance as nonscientific healing recovers importance where scientific medicine has not served. Like Latin and Greek and the rest of the "classical" curriculum for gentlemen, they thus would become the cut-flower components of the vocationally rooted culture which displaces them. Their continued existence and visibility would turn alone on the vocation of specialists and their transmission by the learned to an otiose elite. The aficionados of their economy will then complain of decadence and materialism and prophesy doom.

VI

I come now to the issue which Dean Henle raises—that I tend "to regard Americanism as an ultimate ideology," to make it a "surrogate religion," and to identify it with "cultural relativism," significantly replacing my own word, "pluralism," with this other, "relativism." [4] This demands "uniformity of ideology" and ignores the essential distinction between "accepting" individual human beings and "approving their ideas." It would, if imposed, "place once again before the religious conscience a choice of God *or* Caesar." My interpretation "deprives pluralism—in the crucial field of ideology—of substantial reality and thus by an apparent paradox cultural relativism results in an ideological monism." If accepted, "Americanism would be turned into a persecuting pressure, forcing a conformity in philosophical relativism."

This interpretation of cultural pluralism strikes me as yet one more *Tu quoque* currently in vogue among the authoritarians and dogmatists whose views Dean Henle here bespeaks with distinguished clearness, distinctness and charm. Another version of them asserts that the First Amendment to the Constitution is theological by implication, obliging Americans to believe that all churches are simply voluntary societies, with none preferred by God over the others, and that it thus "canonizes liberal Protestant ecclesiology in an extreme form and anathematizes as un-American all dissenters." Yet since this is itself a dissent freely and safely propagated under the protection of the First Amendment, and propagated on behalf of the claims of a dogmatism which suppresses similar dissents wherever its aficionados command the power, its mere existence demonstrates its factitiousness. It is not a review and summary of the relevant actualities. It is a dialectical miracle transmuting a *de jure* and *de facto* pluralism into an "ideological monism" because of the obvious fact that a Many can and do freely join together and separate, agree and disagree in any and every way save that which would destroy their equal freedom to do so.

From the standpoint of a bona fide pluralism, mankind's

---

[4] As I use it, this word signifies only recognition of and assent to the actuality of relations. But the obstinate historic endeavor to subject the Many to a One of the endeavorer's own choice has rendered "relativism" an explosive emotion-charged word. I wish there were an apter, more sedative replacement to signify the actualities of relation between persons, places, beliefs, events, thoughts and things, their stases and their mobilities. I have been wondering about "relationalism."

"ultimate ideologies" are many, not one. Each is an individual configuration of beliefs different from every other. The faithful of each tend to claim that it and it alone is the true one, and hence entitled to exclusive consideration and privileges. The resulting relationships between the different companies of believers are contingent on these conflicting claims. Yet apart from the minds and hearts of the believers whose "ultimate ideologies" are these configurations, they obtain as arrangements of signs and symbols into statements about the present, past and future of events and objects other than themselves, expressing, in Dean Henle's phrase, "the fundamental meaning of the world and of human life." Whenever a person so apprehends them that he is said to be convinced of them, they figure as the convictions of his head and heart. Western religions usually designate certain such convictions as articles of faith, and becoming convinced of them as conversion. They are the convert's substance of things hoped for, his evidence of things not seen.

But they are this substance and evidence not by virtue of what they are in themselves, their being or their essence, but by virtue of the act of faith which transvalues them into convictions. We know that people freely withdraw their faith from one set of articles and commit themselves to a different set. We know that evangelists, missionaries, propagandists, inquisitors, brain-washers, advertisers, educators, are persons whose vocation it is to procure such changes of conviction by persuasion, by coercion, or both. We know also, how, before the ongoing democratic revolution of our time began, dogmatists everywhere in Europe and the Americas imposed cruel penalties on people whose "ultimate ideologies" were different from their own. We know with what inhumanities they compelled the different to forsake their own "ultimate ideologies" and not alone "approve" but commit themselves to the "ultimate ideology" of their torturers. Those who do not so, but give up their lives for their faith, we call martyrs. There are, of course, persons with power whose inhumanities are means to other ends than making converts to their professed "ultimate ideology." Those are not presently relevant. It is the believers who practice their inhumanities sincerely and only for the sake of such conversions that signify here.

We call them fanatics. This is the difference between the martyr and the fanatic: that the martyr sacrifices only his own life
for his conscience, while the fanatic sacrifices only other
people's lives for his conscience; that the martyr resists the
ultima ratio regum to his own death, while the fanatic mobi-
lizes it to bring death to others. With the martyr the forced
option becomes *My* God, *my* "ultimate ideology" or *my* life,
while with the fanatic the option forced is *My* God, *my* "ultimate ideology," or *Your* life. In either case, the "ultimate
ideology" is an ultimatum which the fanatic presents and the
martyr rejects, exposing himself to the *ultima ratio* of the coercive force strong and cunning to penalize him for his ob-
durate dissent in every degree, from fines and silencing,
through segregation, banishment, incarceration, torture and
auto da fé.

The relationships signified by the words "martyr," "fanatic"
gain increasing visibility wherever, in a diversified society, a
group become aggressive about their "ultimate ideology" and
enjoin it on other people on pains and penalties. Civilization
abounds in instances of such aggressions and their consequences. The freer societies of our own time have hardly
finished defending themselves against one of them—the Nazis'
crusade on behalf of their "ultimate ideology" of racism; the
same societies are in the midst of a cold war waged by another
—the Communists' crusade on behalf of their "ultimate ideology" of dialectical materialism. Here in the United States,
Americans converted to that "ultimate ideology" have been
free, under the protection of the Constitution, to form groups
and parties, to teach and preach and argue this conviction of
theirs "about the fundamental meaning of the world and of
human life," until it became evident that all this was one phase
of a fanatical aggression constituting a clear and present danger
to the liberties and safety of the American people. Other
Americans, with a tradition of commitment to an "ultimate
ideology" of "white supremacy," carry on still a fanatical
aggression against dark-skinned fellow Americans, martyrizing
them for that difference in every degree of cruelty from segregation to sadistic slaughter.

Their fanaticisms wage a war against the American Idea
which some justify as a war for God against Caesar. And why?

Precisely because "Caesar" here signifies an "ultimate ideology," according to which non-Communists and Negroes, together with such "ultimate ideologies" as they are jointly and severally committed to, are, equally with Communists and Whitists, endowed with unalienable rights to life, liberty, and the pursuit of happiness; rights which governments are instituted to secure. If Dean Henle's argument has any merit it would follow that political and legal measures taken to defend the liberties of non-Communists and Negroes from the fanaticism of Communists and Whitists constitute "a persecuting pressure forcing conformity in philosophical relativism."

For all which, in theory and practice, "conformity to philosophical relativism" can here signify, is conformity to the right not to conform, that is, conformity to freedom.[5] Indeed, Theodore Parker, who originated the symbolic expression, "American Idea," offers the "idea of freedom" as a synonym for it.

I do not at this time raise the question of the *what* and *how* of an "ultimate ideology" of freedom, or of the role of freedom in other "ultimate ideologies" than of freedom. I wish now, in connection with some other issues Dean Henle raises, to call attention to certain historical data and contemporary situations. The first regards the Declaration of Independence. It does, as any reader may note, contain a series of propositions regarding "the fundamental meaning of the world and of human life." Above all, the propositions attribute freedom, together with life and the pursuit of happiness, to the original nature of the whole man. They base government and its authority on this freedom, through the consent of the free. They oppose consent to coercion. The peoples of the original thirteen colonies had suffered coercion not only from British power across the sea, but also at one another's hands in almost

[5] In his essay on Liberty, John Stuart Mill has set down the classical exposition of the theory and practice of this freedom with respect also to "ultimate ideologies," including the ultimate ideology of freedom, and how its denial requires its affirmation. I hold Mill's essay to be one (and here a very relevant one) amplification of the American Idea in relation to the diverse and diversifying multitude of "fundamental meanings of the world and of human life." For this reason I call attention to it here, recommend its study to all concerned with the dynamics of the cultures and intercultural relations, but say no more about it save to thank Dean Henle for providing me with the occasion to refer to it.

every dimension of their life together—political and economic
as well as religious, and it continues ominous among their
epigons. At last they affirmed and exercised their unalienable
rights as free men to resist, to alter and abolish the cause of
their suffering. Among the signers of the Declaration were believers in the "ultimate ideologies" of the major denominations
of Christians, including the Roman Catholic; there were also
Quakers and Unitarians and Deists. All of them pledged to
the support of the Declaration their lives, their fortunes and
their sacred honors. They bet their whole existence on its
terms, and that wager perforce had to cover each one's existence as a believer in this or that "ultimate ideology." Their
several ideologies were stakes of their joint wager.

During the interregnum between the winning of the wager
and the adoption of the Constitution and the Bill of Rights,
there occurred irruptions of the warfare between "ultimate
ideologies" with its poles of fanaticism and martyrdom, and
the warfare continues potential among the diverse organizations defining themselves by their "ultimate ideologies."

"Of all the animosities which have existed among mankind,"
declared George Washington, "those which are caused by
differences of sentiments in religion appear to be the most
inveterate and distressing, and ought most to be deprecated."
Who doubts that he spoke the consensus of the Founding
Fathers? The American Idea very soon took on the aspect of
an implicit covenant between Americans to assure the life and
liberty of each from the aggression of any. The Virginia
Bill for Religious Liberty is a representative implementation
of this consensus, with its emphasis on the First Amendment
and the separation of church and state. Commitment to these
alters the relations between societies of ultimate ideologists
from fanatical aggression against one another to free and
peaceful competition with one another to hold and win converts, and on occasion to pool and share their diversities as
means to common ends of ideological peace. Such peace is a
declared end, for example, of the National Conference of
Christians and Jews, stated in their by-laws thus:

"To promote justice, amity, understanding and co-operation
among Protestants, Catholics, and Jews, and to analyze, moderate
and finally eliminate intergroup prejudices which disfigure and

distort religious, business, social, and political relations, with a view to the establishment of a social order in which the religious ideals of brotherhood and justice shall become the standards of human relationships."

Here is confirmation of Mr. Stewart Cole's reservation, to his very generous agreement with the perceptions and principles set forth in this study. His reservation regards the contribution of authoritarians and dogmatists to betterment in our free spiritual and social economy, and how they often do fruitfully work together with holders of contrasted "ultimate ideologies." It was not my intention to ignore or belittle these data. I have not, however, found them to bulk large in the record. That indicates rather that fundamentalists, whatever their communion, tend either to decline all association with the different, or wage a cold war against them, or join them for some differential profit to themselves alone. The last look back to an assumption which guides all varieties of enterprise; its apt symbol is the phrase, "What is good for General Motors is good for the country." James Madison drew the logical and practical consequences of this assumption for the freedoms of a free society in the tenth paper of *The Federalist*. The ratio of such as freely collaborate is small, and the collaboration, where it occurs, is an exemplification of the American Idea at work in the hearts of the collaborators.

Have we not, now, indication enough of the terms of the "ultimate ideology" which the American Idea signalizes? And what are the interpersonal, interfaith and intercultural consequences of conversion to it? It does not need defense on the ideological level because it is the only defense from one another's aggression which aficionados of the many "ultimate ideologies" have to depend upon. Far from needing to be "adjustable to these ideologies," government, as the works implementing the faith which is the American Idea, is charged with the responsibility of assuring that the ideologies are adjusted to one another's freedom and that none breaks the peace by practicing aggression against any. Of course, then, the Idea isn't a "surrogate" to any religion. Nor is it a substitute for all. It is that apprehension of human nature and human relations, which every sort and condition of Protestant, Catholic, Judaist, Moslem, Buddhist, and every other communion m·

agree upon, be converted to and convinced of, if they mean to live freely and peacefully together as equals, none penalizing the others for his otherness and all insuring each the equal protection of the law. And this is how the American Idea is, literally, religion.

Since, however, the word "religion" is another of our explosive, emotion-charged words, it is appropriate to point out again that, as religion, the American Idea is not a One, supervening upon and displacing a Many it emerges from. Nor is it a competing alternative to any other one religion. Its role is to confirm to each its equal liberty to live and to grow among all. It embodies an "ultimate ideology" of *how* different "ultimate ideologies" actually assure to themselves and to one another "domestic tranquillity and the blessings of liberty." It defines the way that different and otherwise incommunicado religions can and do share religion with one another.

And this is why I feel that in relation to the American Idea, Dean Henle's hypothetical option, *God or Caesar*, seems to me a purely verbal one. For in this connection what is Caesar, who is Caesar? If he is but the symbol of the consensus of the different cults to learn, to recognize, to respect, to communicate and to appreciate each other's singularities, to work together wherever possible, and to agree peacefully to disagree where not, no option can arise. The only possible option would be one between God and God, imposed by the fanatical aggression of one religious society against the equal liberty and similar exclusive claims of the others. Then "Caesar" would signify the gathering of the others to defend the freedom and safety of their own beliefs and works and ways.

The cultivation of these, the tendance of their growth, exfoliation and refinement is, when the believers feel sure of being safe and free, their true vocation. Each communion then figures as maintainer and producer of values which enter into the culture of other communions whose vocation is to produce values singular to their own "ultimate ideology." The culture of each is diversified, nourished and enriched from the vocation of the others.

Where an economy of cultural abundance exists, it is postulated on these differences of vocation, these diversities of labor, in every domain of the human enterprise, in religion quite as much as in industry, the arts, the sciences and literature. When a producer seeks to make his vocation the only one in the field, and his faith sole and alone the "ultimate ideology" of all men, the economy of religion contracts into an economy of spiritual scarcity which extends to the other dimensions of the culture wherein the religion lives and moves and has its being. As a verse of Abu El-Yezdi's "Kasidah" has it, Englished by Sir Richard Burton.

> All faith is false, all faith is true;
> Truth is the shattered mirror strown
> In myriad bits; while each believes
> His little bit the whole to own.

Abundance, to say nothing of completeness, is impossible without pluralism. Scarcity is impossible without monism. Variety is not only the spice of life, it is the life of life. In a pluralistic society whose culture is *unum in pluribus*, dogmatists and their dogmas actually hold a place even as the open-minded and their postulates. But no more than so. It is no problem for a bona fide cultural pluralist to enter into fruitful open and peaceful communication with the one and to understand and appreciate the other. His problem is created when the dogmatist undertakes to transpose this morality of free communication into the morality of prescriptive indoctrination, when he assumes to impose his dogma. Then, if the pluralist's defense against such aggression is not to be a counter-aggression, he must resort to the American Idea to restore the morality of freedom, and thus vindicate to each "ultimate ideology" the collective assurance of its individual ultimacies.

I have done. It now remains to thank my friends and critics for their kindness in taking the trouble to read my essay, and for their courteous and helpful consideration of its argument.